The Voice of My Heart
*Unforgettable Memories
in an Unforgettable Year*

The Voice of My Heart

Unforgettable Memories in an Unforgettable Year

Edited by Merna Ann Hecht
Introduced by Merna Ann Hecht & Carrie Stradley
Foreword by Shahrzad Shams

Poetry and Art from the 2021-22 Stories of Arrival:
Refugee & Immigrant Youth Voices Poetry Project

Cover Art: Suan D. Pau, from Burma
Graphic Design: Richard Rogers
Photography: David Lynch

Stories of Arrival: Refugee and Immigrant Youth Voices Poetry Project
is powered by Shunpike.
Shunpike is the 501(c)(3) non-profit agency that provides independent arts
groups in Washington State with the services, resources, and opportunities
they need to forge their own paths to sustainable success.

ISBN: 978-1-63405-042-5
Library of Congress Control Number: 2022937433

Limited Edition Published on behalf of the Stories of Arrival: Refugee &
Immigrant Youth Voices Poetry Project, 2023. All proceeds from the sale of
this book benefit projects for refugee and immigrant youth.

This book is dedicated to the brave refugee and immigrant poets who fill its pages with the voices of their hearts—voices in search of a world where all belong and all can live safely in a place they call home.

May their longing for a time when peace prevails be the work we all undertake.

FOREWORD

This visionary project serves our community with a peace-making ambassadorship. Over the course of its years, since 2009, the Stories of Arrival Project has created a community of poets, readers and listeners to bear witness to the unfathomable stories of young refugees touched by the scourge of war and displacement.

Merna Hecht and Carrie Stradley have opened a way for enduring transformations by holding the space between grief and rebirthing that honors the identity and reality of these young poets. What a joy it is to witness how the redemptive magic of poetry reveals the resilience of the spirit of these young people, many who have arrived here from unimaginably difficult circumstances.

These poems are honest, tender and vulnerable like their writers and they offer us uncensored accounts of history. There is a lesson in each, and an awakening call to become better human beings.

I am an immigrant of half a century with a yearning in my heart for the home I left behind. These young poets planted a flower in that empty space with each and every poem, turning the barren into a life-giving garden, a place to come to, to cherish the memories of what no longer is, and to plant what can be.

Reading the poems will touch your heart in profound ways as they take you intimately on a journey. They grab our attention and softly hold our hands while they whisper into our ears, truths about our own realities. How redemptive to hold each other's words in the sacred space of our shared humanity.

We, the readers can be the community that bears witness to these told and untellable stories. Read these poems to enrich your spirit. Read them again to honor the spirit of humanity, the force of which is strong in these young poets. Read them out loud so the oral history of these young people are heard widely in our world where they are desperately needed.

Shahrzad Shams
Assistant Teaching Professor, Persian and Iranian Studies
Department of Near Eastern Languages and Civilization
University of Washington, Seattle, WA
Executive Director of Peyvand, A Community Non-profit
Organization in Support of Immigrants

INTRODUCTION

Merna Ann Hecht

I begin with a tribute to each young person in this year's Stories of Arrival Poetry Project which took place during this unforgettable year of ongoing pandemic, school closures and enormous world-wide challenges. The effect of the pandemic on the lives of students locally and globally has taken a lasting toll. Yet, the young people in this year's project prevailed. Even as they were acutely aware of threats to loved ones in their home countries because of climate related drought, extreme food scarcity and violent conflicts, they welcomed poetry into their lives, honoring its mysterious abilities to express their heart's truths. They wrote of their memories, creating vulnerable openings into their experiences of leave-taking and arrivals. They rose to the challenge of searching for words to express in English what they know intimately in their mother tongue. I am grateful that several of the poets placed home languages within their poems or have gifted us with full translations.

On their behalf, I ask you to keep in mind that our anthology is not meant for reading beginning to end. Rather, open it to any section or skip to the back to meet these young adults who have arrived in their new home from seventeen different countries. Let your eyes rest on a colorful image; let your heart travel with a young man or woman in leave of his or her homeland. Let a poem about the scents and stories that fill a home kitchen and define a shared meal bring you to your own remembered spices and tastes of home.

I invite you to allow yourself to grapple with the pressing issues of our time in company with the courage of these young poets. As you read, you will find lived experiences and intergenerational knowledge of the horrors of war and genocide along with poems that reveal betrayals to basic human rights as if they were something to offer to some and withhold from others. You will repeatedly come across the shared anguish of leaving a beloved homeland. It is *shared* because the generosity in these poems is always beyond the writer. These young poets speak for all children's safety, for all who have had to leave home, for all who hunger, for all countries to know peace. They write past their own sorrows or struggles with an embrace of kindness toward all the earth and its inhabitants, human and non-human.

Througout the book, especially in the last section, you will find poems that offer a wide lens into the awareness that each young person in the project holds regarding the harm visited on the plants, animals and exquisite beauty of the natural world. Like many of their age, our poets are deeply concerned about climate matters and they are also truth tellers speaking out against the irreversible damage that comes from occupying armies, violent dictators and the abject greed for money and power, all sadly part of our world. But, not the only part, because in each section you will find the determined wings of the peace dove aloft and flying through these poems.

In late February, just as I began editing and co-designing this book, Russia launched the invasion of Ukraine furthering the uncertainty and global instability with which we live. My gratitude for immersing in poems that uphold the vision of a world where we might live in harmony, expressed by the poets in this year's project, became a source of unanticipated solace. Along with this vision, they also express their understanding of the wrenching displacements, irreparable destruction and tragic loss of life that occur on all sides of violent conflicts. They remind us how we must stand strong for people of every ethnicity and skin color who are forced to flee from inhumane conditions. Writing poetry has asked much of these young people and in turn they are asking us to actively abhor war wherever it occurs.

It is an honor and privilege to have befriended and learned from the young people in this year's project. From poems expressing the lilting and simple delight of waking up near the sea in Vietnam to take in the colors of the sunrise, to the lingering sorrow of missing a mother and a motherland, or the profound injustice for migrants cruelly detained in Libya, or the trafficking of young women, these poets bring us face to face with the daring of hope and the reality of our deepest collective flaws. I am humbled by their understanding. To me, their words read like a form of prayer.

Hope for a better world speaks and sings through the voices of these young poets. It is the hope for the future they deserve and it is the world they can create should their voices reach far and wide.

Merna Ann Hecht
Project Founder, Co-Director, Editor and Teaching Artist for Poetry
April, 2022

INTRODUCTION

Carrie Stradley

This years' book is aptly titled, as it has indeed been a remarkable year for the Stories of Arrival Youth poets. I often wonder how the students will look back on this global pandemic- in masks, physically distanced, contact traced, while living through news of war and hunger, climate change and political tensions. For now, the answer lies in the lines and stanzas of their poems. Students wrote from their lived experiences, read each other's lives in lines, revised to find new ways of seeing, spoke out loud what was quietly awaiting an audience, and grew as a community. Their voices, their points of view are expressed clearly and with an honesty that sounds the alarm for what wars and climate change have done to our planet and to so many people. In their poems, a far-away war isn't far away anymore. The remnants of loss are in stories that travel off the pens of our students. The poets also spoke lovingly and longingly of their cultures back home, as they navigate what it means to live in this new country. More than anything, this anthology stands as a document in time, giving us an opportunity to bear witness and honor the lives of these youth.

Throughout the Project and this school year, I have watched my students grow in their willingness to share of themselves, in their command of the English language, and how they react to the world around them. No single test can demonstrate this so vividly and beautifully.

Working so closely for all of these years with poet and social justice advocate and teacher Merna Ann Hecht, has reinforced the power that poetry holds. The delicate balance of holding one's deepest pain and proudest joy while gently unfolding it all into a poem is not an easy task. Teaching alongside Ms. Merna has made the art and craft of poetry a beautiful and necessary learning for all of us, and I thank her for that immensely.

And you, reader, I also thank you. Thank you for joining us in honoring our youth poets. Their perspective is necessary and vital. This Project uses poetry to transport culture and transcend time, serving to record humanity in history. Thank you for joining us on our Stories of Arrival.

Carrie Stradley
Project Co-Director, Foster High School, MLL Teacher,
National Board Certified Teacher

POETRY IS

Poetry is the wind outside,
and the morning prayer you offer to the sun.
Poetry is my voice when I feel like I have none
and the sound of lightning and the sound of city buses.

Poetry is a poem that comes from your heart like a tree dancing
with the air, and it is the sun rising in the morning.

Poetry is a beautiful history,
it is a strong voice that comes from the heart, it touches
the heart and you can hear your heart reading poetry.

Poetry is the waves that show your mood or feelings,
it is the color of the moonlight,
and the feeling of listening to music you like
and the feeling of cold air.

Poetry is a mystery or riddle to solve,
it is beautiful like the girl I like,
and it is the beauty of love.

Poetry is the voice of my feelings when I'm sad,
it is like a ship in time, it makes you travel the world
without movement.

I hear the word poetry and I think of painting,
poetry is a gift.

Poetry is a glass of water in winter and the sound of thunder
when it's cloudy and rainy.

Poetry is the home language of my heart and the taste
of my mother's handmade food.

Poetry is rain which makes flowers alive and awake
and it is a burst of light shining on someone.

Poetry is a pen that can write the future
and a pencil that can write good and bad memories.

Poetry is the voice of my feelings when I'm sad,
and it is a wind that goes everywhere,
and poetry is a welcome world to everyone.

Poetry could be yourself in third person,
it is a book where I can express my feelings,
and a beautiful place, where I can live in freedom
and hear the sound of the truth in my heart.

Poetry is like a candle which enlightens others' lives,
it is the tears when I remember my homeland,
and it is the noise of the chickens in the early morning
waking everyone up to pray.

Poetry is like stars in the dark night,
poetry is flying over the ocean,
it is the smell of my grandma's fresh bread,
and it is like eating shawarma in the morning.

Poetry is the spirit of my life
and the beautiful image of the world.

— Collaborative Poem by the Stories of Arrival Poets

the mood light of Poetry

Poetry and Identity
Who I Am and Where I Come From

Words from Our Poets

~ I am a person with lots of sadness in my heart
because I am an immigrant.
When I listen to other people's poems their suffering
and their humor inspires and transforms me.

~ Now I know how to sympathize and understand better
with my friends. More than that is learning how to help
others speak their "voice" in their hearts. The sound of tears
flowing back when they were most lonely and desperate, the
sound of hearts fluttering when found.

~ Poetry connects people by holding mysterious words
of the people's identity and it is easy to imagine the
beautiful sounds of the words.

Unforgettable Memories

I come from a small village, Bossango,
in the Central African Republic near Bangui City
from many immigrant refugees
who traveled to have a better life with their parents
away from small villages.
I will not forget leaving friends behind in the village,
leaving behind my friend, Saleh,
the friend I spent all of my days with.

I will not forget the war in my country
and the many who lost their lives,
the children who lost their parents,
and parents who lost their children.
I will not forget the refugee camp in *Tchad
inside its dark forests
standing next to scared parents.

I will not forget that I am from a place of refuge
that turned into a place of war,
from those forests
where people cried for help,
like sheep,
crying for their lives.

I will not forget my long journey to the United States
when I was eighteen years old.
Though I am starting my education,
I miss my friends
and the forests where we played together.

I will never forget
that I am from the dark forest of the refugee camp,
and I am from the strong place
in my heart,
and the unforgettable memories of my life
in my small village.

– Ahamat Bire

* French: Tchad for the Republic of Chad

MY MEMORY BOX

My old box full of memories
tells different stories,
stories which show the beauty of my emotions,
like when I was a little girl playing on the beach
making strong buildings from the soft sand,
or when I was a guardian angel working with my grandpa
under the pink sky to grow Mustard flowers
to give to friends and teachers.

I am still the little girl who carries the fragrance
of my country's soil in my hand,
the little girl who makes utensils
from soil for her dolls.

Now, I am the rainy sky who cries over old memories
all night in the youthful new year,
and I am a fresh new morning
after the dust is cleaned from the air.

I am the music in the air
who makes the trees dance in the winter.
I am the loud waves who play *kabaddi*
with children in the summer.

Inside of my memory box I am
the incomplete puzzle,
who is still looking for missing pieces.
I am an incomplete song
who is still looking for those
missing lyrics.

– NILA SAFI

THE CHILD I WAS

I was the child
who smiled when she flew
from Kenya to Somalia
to meet her sister, brother and grandmother
for the first time.

I was the child
who didn't have many friends
who looked down and spoke in tiny voices
mostly with her brothers.

I was the child
who spent all day crying
when her mother took her to school
because she would rather play with sand
than read or write.

I am the young woman
who feels scared
for the nine-year-old girls
who lost their parents,
who run from men
who force themselves
on these young girls,
and a system that
does not punish the men
for their actions.

I am the young woman
who wants to live a life
without fighting, killing, stealing,
without destroying homes and bodies,
who wants to dream
of children who live in a magical universe
like little children should.

- HAFSO SHEIKOMAR

FROM MY CHILDHOOD

I am the child who grew up in a little town,
San Lorenzo in El Salvador.

I am the child that grew up eating the traditional food,
smelling the fresh coffee in the morning,
looking at the river between the mountains.

I am the child that left his country when he was only twelve,
the child who left his other self,
who left the past
and the lessons of respect for the child
who follows the right future.

I am the child who lost his grandparents
when he left the country,
a country that has freedom and good people.

I am the child who will work as hard as he can
to make his grandparents proud,
the child who will never forget his grandma,
the woman who always told him,
siempre mira para un mejor future.

I am the child who will never forget
his grandparents,
the ones who taught him the word respect.
I am the child who will never give up with the promise
made to them that he would choose the right path.

– LUIS ORELLANA MENDOZA

My Memories

I am a young woman who holds memories of her past life,
living in a refugee camp with her family
all together and crowded
with the sounds of mothers talking about their children.

I am a young woman who cares about her people in Somalia
who have been living in war, destruction, and poverty
for more than three decades,
who hopes that her country will live peacefully one day.

I am a young woman who dreams of becoming a doctor
to take care of people who are dying
at the hands of wars around the world.

I am a young woman who dreams.

– Keyrun Osman

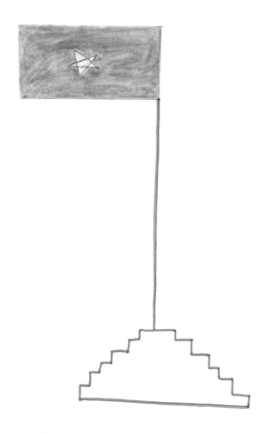

A Girl with Dreams

I am a girl with dreams, but with fears at the same time.
I am a daughter with wishes never to see her mother tired again.
I am a sincere girl who in my heart has only love to show.
I am a girl who loves and falls in love over and over again.
I am a girl who once cried herself to sleep, but now smiles at what is coming.
I am a girl who loves to dance and feels free to the rhythm of music.
I am the best creation of God.
I am what I speak.
I am what surrounds me.
I am what I feel.
I am what you do not see.

- Perla Del Rosario Garcia Moro

THE LAND OF ERITREA

Eritrea, the place I am from
my beloved country,
land of fresh air and beautiful nature,
warm in summer and cold in winter
with square hail that hits you on your head.

I remember the green plants growing under the rain,
I remember the beautiful surroundings in my neighborhood,
green trees with blooming flowers and scents of *ryhan*.

I remember you with your giant mountains
that lose people like in an endless maze,
and I remember your sandy ground.

I am what I am,
the little boy who once lived in a small village with his mom,
tending his family's sheep in the early morning,
and going to the mosque at night.
I am a quiet, respectful young man
with a light shining in his eyes
to go back to his home,
to his friends, to his grandma,
to the kind country and people he misses.

بلادي الحسنة الحرب مزقتها
وكل يوم طبول الحرب تقرع
حرب قديمة منذ الأزل
مع الجيران او داخل الوطن
روحي ودمي فداء لوطني بعزالله
فكل يوم لبلدي اشتاق وذلي سلامها احلم

- BESSAM MOHAMMAD

THIS GREEN LAND

My beautiful country, Ethiopia,
your proud flag
green, yellow, and red
a blue star shining in the middle.
Your land of seemingly opposing religions,
Christianity and Islam that live together
with no hate.

I am from this green land,
covered in ancient civilization
who fought with other countries
but was never colonized.

I honor this green land with deep jungles,
with waters that connect us to other countries.
I am from this country
who needs to fight together for one goal,
to work together,
to build us up from the bottom,
to tell the whole and complete story
of Ethiopia.

- ANAWAR KIMO

A Young Man from The Gambia

My country The Gambia, West Africa
is full of many languages,
Mandinka, Wolof, Jola, Manjogo, Fula, Aku, and Soninke,
everyone speaking peacefully together.

I miss visiting my family members
speaking our shared language,
I miss how we all understand each other
and laugh together,
my sister's laugh so loud
it echoes and fills the neighborhood.

I am a young man with gratitude for my family
gently guided by my brothers and sisters,
with my sister's explanation and help
I learned to guide myself.

I remember the long days going to the Palma Rima beach
swimming in the warm water of the ocean
and after, playing football with my friends, Yankuba and Yano.

I am a young Gambian man with a love for reading the Quran
with my Muslim brothers and sisters
offering us help and teaching its lessons.
I am from thanking God that I can learn
and read our sacred texts.

I am a young man with dreams
of achieving my goals,
always working towards them,
knowing what it means to graduate
with good credits to go to college and university,
and being able to support my parents
thankful for their constant love,
trying to do as they say
giving and getting respect.

– Mohamed Lamin Ceesay

THE ONE WHO LEFT DUSTY STREETS

I am a young man
born in a city called Keren,
a city that sits next to the Red Sea
with warm and cloudy days.

I am the young man who faced problems in his life
but found a way and learned from his mistakes.
I am a student of respect
who listens to his elders and follows the rules.

I am the son of a farmer who grew
guava, lettuce, corn and oranges
to sell at the market.

I am the one who left dusty streets
and the invitations from strangers
to hunt for his future
to succeed in a new country
because he couldn't remain in his homeland.

I am someone who tries to help others
to show honor and respect.
I am someone who tries to make their life easier
because he knows helping each other
brings happiness.

– ANES MOHAMMAD

MY LAND OF COLORFUL HIJABS AND WIDE SMILES

I come from Djibouti,
a land of colorful hijabs and wide smiles,
a land covered with soft sand
touched by turquoise ocean.

I am from one sister, Asma,
and four brothers; Abass, Khalid,
Kadar and Ahmed.

I long for the smell of home,
soft injera and green pepper stuffed
inside Sambusa.

I am from the hope
that everyone should clean our ocean
and come together
so that animals stay safe
and plants thrive.

I come from making black tea on weekends,
 crushing cardamom, pounding ginger, adding sugar,
boiling on the stove and serving it to my auntie,
then my mom and grandma tell me *waanu jecenlnahay shaahaage,*
Somali for *"I love your tea."*

– FATOUMA ABDI

He Who Sees Himself as a Ghost Traveling

He who struggled to learn English in school, when he came to America
after leaving the Kakuma refugee camp,
He who remembers leaving his big sister in Kenya,
He who remembers the sweet smell of leftover sambusa
in the mornings of Ramadan.
He who misses the wide oceans of Somalia
and the smell of injera,
He who sees himself as a ghost traveling
around the world learning new things, seeing new places.
He who desires to help people in need,
He who remembers the war in his country,
He who remembers the day he left his homeland because of the war,
He who saw families leave loved ones behind,
He who dreams of peace in his homeland.

– Mustaf Osman

He Who Remembers

He who remembers the sound of a river calling his name,
He who travels as far us a river and never stops,
He who can see the wind with the smell of flowers,
He who remembers his home in El Salvador,
He who can see a tree falling in the forest,
He who can see the deep ocean,
He who can remember the love of his mother and her truth.

– Luis Orellana Mendoza

My Lovely Sonora

I am a young man from the top of Mexico
where people cross the border
in darkness to avoid being seen.

I am from the rain not falling
where soft sand flies,
and where fishing is abundant
at certain times of the year.

I remember people traveling from far away
to eat our *Popeyes hamburguesas y tacos de birria,*
made with *carne de res*
and the tastes of the best *carnes asadas y tortillas de harina*
made in small outside *puertecitos*
where those *puertecitos* are lined up
along our earthen streets.

I remember our Sunday streets
long with *tianguis*
selling their juicy red *granadas,*
and bright green *guamuchiles*, and pink filled *guava.*

I remember the fireworks
lighting the night sky on Christmas Eve
and the sounds of gunshots covering the sky
marking the New Year.

I come from the kindness of people
asking, *"Te sientes bien?"*
where people will tell you,
"No hagas eso si te miro asienlo
otra vez le voy a decir a tu mama,"
where people treat you like family
even if you're not part of the family, you are.

I come from asking and receiving,
from neighbors who gladly help,
where we played hide and seek in the dark
without a worry of our safety.

I was among those neighborhood children
playing from sunrise to after the setting of the sun,
knowing everyone in my neighborhood,
this place I am from
where family and friends come first.

– Isaac Padilla

I Am What I Am

I am of the purity of my mother,
I am like a piece of glass, fragile but shiny.
I am a woman with feelings, fragile as the flutter of innocence,
sometimes I think that the things inside destroy the things on the outside
as if wanting to be myself were a sin that deserves punishment.
I am the one who enjoys the happiness of others
and conforms to the darkness of the night,
an area where the white dove never flies,
where Chernobyl and her elephant leg fall short.
I am the one who is full of emptiness,
but at least I have metrics, I am filled with defects,
astral travel feelings
I wear out on the way
I lost life and lost time.
I am the one who does not have reviews,
because nobody thinks of visiting my
avenue of disaster.
You can call me insensitive, you can call a coward,
I am a free lamb, God save me from the flock.

- Jenifer Carrera Garrido

I Am

I am a young girl whose quiet voice belongs to me,
who feels shy to share my ideas.
I am a young girl who misses
her grandmother and grandfather, Bon va Phuong
who she left behind in Vietnam.
I am a young girl who misses her
grandmother's cooking
Bun Bo Hue soup like pho,
a bowl of beef broth waiting for my hands.

I am a young girl with memories from my childhood,
playing games and laughing with my friends
Thien, Nhu and Hien after school.

I am a young girl who longs for
the day she will return to Dalat City,
to the people-filled streets and sidewalk cafes,
the eateries around the small streets,
and the chilly sky of Dalat City
holding a cup of hot soy milk served
with delicious cakes and unforgettable memories.

I am a young girl who hopes Vietnam can develop further
and hopes that many tourists can come to Vietnam to visit
and experience my country's culture.

– Uyen Cill-Pame

TÔI LÀ AI

Tôi là một cô gái trẻ có giọng nói trầm lắng thuộc về tôi
Ai cảm thấy ngại chia sẻ ý kiến của tôi
Em là một cô bé nhớ bà ngoại và ông ngoại Bốn và Phường .
Ai cô ấy đã bỏ lại ở Việt Nam
Tôi là một cô gái trẻ nhớ cô ấy
bà ngoại tôi nấu món bún bò huế rất ngon
Bún bò Huế như phở
Tô nước dùng bò chờ tay em.

Tôi là một cô gái trẻ với những kỷ niệm từ thời thơ ấu của tôi,
chơi trò chơi và cười
Với các bạn Thiện, Như, Hiền
Sau giờ học

Tôi là một cô gái trẻ khao khát
Ngày cô ấy sẽ trở lại thành phố Đà Lạt
Đến những con đường chật cứng người và những quán cà phê vỉa hè
Những quán ăn quanh những con phố nhỏ
Trời se lạnh của thành phố Đà Lạt cầm ly sữa đậu nành nóng hổi.
Với những chiếc bánh thơm ngon và những kỉ niệm khó quên
Tôi là một cô gái trẻ mong cho đất nước Việt Nam có thể phát triển hơn nữa
Và mong rằng sẽ có nhiều du khách đến Việt Nam tham quan
Và trải nghiệm văn hóa của đất nước.

– UYEN CILL-PAME

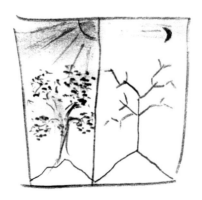

Like a Bird

He who remembers the taste of being in danger,
He who remembers traveling far for a better life,
He who remembers mistakes he made in life,
He who is like a bird flying out of a cage,
He who remembers the nature of his homeland,
He who remembers the sound of chickens cackling in the early morning,
He who is a person who hates betrayal the most.

– Phubodin Nacharoen

Ho Chi Minh City

Ho Chi Minh City,
where I grew up,
a place that is rarely quiet,
the streets filled with loud motorbikes,
the sounds of bicycle bells
and shouting of people selling
ice creams, fried corn, tofu dishes, and home tools
with the awesome sight of delivery drivers balancing
mattresses, or crates of water, or gas
on the backs of hundreds of motorbikes,
and sometimes waking up to crashing sounds
of cars colliding,
which wasn't surprising.

Ho Chi Minh City with sidewalk eateries,
scents of meat,
pork ribs of the broken rice dish,
the smell of beef bones and greasy beef fat
in the pot of pho
that filled the air when I left the house
for the eatery where we always stopped
on the way home from school,
an eatery whose name I do not know,
but I waited all day for this meal
for those plates of rice, meat and fresh vegetables,
Com Tam, fish sauce, poured over the plate,
left me full, ready to get back on my bicycle
and finish my ride home.

– HOANG NGUYEN

CROSSING MANY LANDS

I am a young man whose name means to encourage growth,
who likes to sketch the natural world in a book like fiction.
I came here from Burma where it's all about farming and gardening,
About houses made of strong bamboo
And clean rivers overflowing on a sunny day
Showing beautiful reflections in the water.
I've crossed land to land, river to river, on foot, and train and boat.
I am a person who went through hardship since I was five,
I am from family immigrating to America for education,
I am a person who works hard to reach my truth.

I am the person behind the shadows.

—SUAN PAU

HE WHO REMEMBERS

He who remembers his grandmother reading a book in the early morning
by the window and the sun bright and shining on her,

He who misses his parents that live far away still in Cambodia,
He who was born with good people of heart who always helped him,
He who remembers when he sat under the trees near the ocean
with his friends listening to music,

He who loves to be kind and respectful to others,

He who remembers playing with butterflies in the garden
in front of his house when the sun almost went down with cold wind,

He who went fishing with his grandpa in the evening on the boat
and the waves pushing the boat around with the noise of the trees
when the wind came.

-HUSNI ZAMIR ASMAT

COUNTRY GROWN

I am the child of a farmer
who loves to feed her animals
and raise chickens, cows, sheep and goats.

I am country grown,
a girl who loves to work on the farm
collecting milk every morning from her cows
to feed her family
from the cows in the meadow
eating beautiful green grass.

I am from those chickens
playing in the meadow with their babies,
some taking long naps in the nest,
some running around chasing other chickens on the farm.

I am the meadow
with little white and yellow flowers
and grass so green,
I am all of us, living on the farm,
the love of cows that give milk
that I can drink,
the chickens that lay eggs for me to eat.

I am what I am, country grown, because of my animals.

– SHARMILA NUR ISLAM

HE WHO WANTS TO HELP

He who wants to prove to everyone
that they were wrong about him.

He who thinks he will help his family
with everything.

He who wants to help homeless people
and poor people who don't have any money
to buy food for his country,
he who wants to help the world.

He who wants to become a pro soccer player.

He who wants to play soccer for his country, Afghanistan
and make the people happy and proud.

He who has a lot of problems in his life,
but never loses hope.

He who likes to be someone different
from others.

He who is working hard to chase his dreams.

ALI SIENA AHMADZADA

A Flower in the Glowing Garden

I am a flower in the glowing garden,
I am from a small home, like a plant holding sturdy roots with soil,
I am from a country that grows sweet onions
and watermelons brimming with juice,
I am from high mountains with treasures,
 gold and gemstones found nowhere else in the world.
I am a child of all those who lived long ago in cramped houses made of mud,
I am from celebrating Eid twice in a year, fasting for Ramadan,
Everyone waiting for *Adhan* to sip the *Rooh afza* and quench their thirst.
I am from the clear water of *Baghlan* running between hills,
I am all those awards I brought from school, hanging on the wall,
shining with the heart of my family.
I am the language of my ancestors spinning around my tongue
like the shadow that follows me everywhere,
I am the blessings of my grandfather, his hand on my head,
a huge smile on his face like a sudden glimpse of sunlight
to the darkest corners of the room.
I am surrounded by the love of my family,
and I want to be an inspiration for my country's future generation.
I am a queen of my own kingdom,
 a kingdom that speaks silently to people with equality and faith.
I am who I am,
a flower in the glowing garden.

– Kalsoom Mehrabb Niazi

Letters and Poems
to My Homeland

Words from Our Poets

~ Leaving your homeland that you were born and grew up in is like leaving your mother and of course no one wants to leave without their mom.
The hard and painful thing about it is you can't choose to go or stay. It's not optional because you have to emigrate for 100 reasons like war, fighting, no work, poverty and hunger with no food for your children.

~ I wrote about those unforgettable moments that will never come back.

~ I missed my country so much and I work hard and chase my dream so I can go back to my Motherland and build my country and help children to be successful in their life and that is my promise to my country.

~ The only option that I had was sharing my story with the world. Since my country was destroyed the question that I asked myself is, how will I honor my country? And the answer to that is writing poetry.

My Story

My country, my beautiful country
I want to return to you,
I want to go home to my language
and to the laughter on your streets.
I want to hear the sounds from the mosque
calling us to prayer,
I want to feel the love and strength of my people.

I miss waiting for nightfall in Aleppo
to see the stars dictate the sky of Syria,
I miss hearing the lovely prayers from the mosque,
I miss the open air of our house where I drank Arabic coffee
in the mornings with the sun rising and the birds singing.
I miss my street where I was the only girl
fighting with so many boys over a ball.

But the war came, the planes came and came
dropping bomb after bomb
onto our streets, onto my street,
people running for their lives,
barely escaping when the bombs fell into the stone wells,
the bombs aimed at the hospital on our street
where I had been so many times because of my illness.

The war came and I saw shooting and dying
we all lost loved ones because of the war.
Now I dream of getting better
I dream of coming home
to my beautiful Syria.

- Ayat Bakour

Letter to My Homeland

My homeland, the mother of pains,
My homeland, from this empty heart I wish for you peace and happiness.
My homeland, my motherland, we are all broken inside for you.
I wish that I can see you again,
I wish that I can see your streets,
I wish I can see the day when your women are educated and successful.
I want to believe the hard times will pass and that you, my homeland,
Afghanistan, will be free.

— Shahram Faizi

LETTER TO MY HOMELAND

I remember my last thoughts when I left my homeland,
my goodbye tears fell on the boundary of my country, Eritrea,
the bus was filled with my people shouting "oww" this is the tip,
the last of the land of our country called Zalambessa.
This was where some of the people began to panic,
while others were crying quietly,
but I did not notice the emotion of what was happening,
I was lost from the time when the bus passed
Senafe where I grew up and spent my loveliest memories
with my aunt Shnash and my grandparents.

I always believed I was a child of Senafe,
it was the root of my love, I was no child of the big city,
where once I lived with my family, where I shared love with them,
where I was educated,
but none of this love or development
could touch my love for my village life
where my ancestors breathed through the land
and my grandparents were deep roots
in the land of my country's birth.

The bus rolled me away and away and I was lost
in the memory of my summers out of the city,
away from the school and back with my grandparents.
The bus rolled me away and my memory flashed back
to my aunt's warm smile and my grand parents' strong histories
where words full of mystery beyond understanding live.

I remembered my Uncle's *tesfa-lem* jokes and my teachers
telling me they will see me tomorrow to present my work,
and my friends in the time when I still did not know
I would disappear from my whole world.
It was as if I was invisible, without a trace,
like an unsolved crime scene, with no one to solve it,
it was all sudden, and these memories were floating on my brain
like the sun in the middle and the planets floating in their orbits.
I fought inside of my mind, wondering
how everything turned out this way.

My thoughts were heavy, my head lay heavy on the windows
of the bus taking me further away,
I closed my eyes and felt like I was falling, losing myself
in a shattering, haunted mirror with nothing I could do
but wait for time and night to turn to the sun.

Oh my sacred homeland, land of bravery,
land of my birth, womb of my people and my heart,
scattered around this earth every Eritrean longs to return
to you for our burial place, for bringing us home.

– TIEDA TSEGAY ARAYA

LETTER FOR MY HOMELAND, AFGHANISTAN

I remember the beautiful sound of *Adhan* (اذان) that I used to hear
five times a day (الله اكبر),
I remember the laughing sound of children in the hallways of apartments,
I remember walking under the long lasting trees
on the sunny days coming back from school,

I remember the sounds of singing birds early in the morning
to awaken us for *Madrassas* (مدرسه),

I remember those days when we used to run away
from the garden after chopping roses,

I remember those cold days when the city used to sleep
under the blanket of snow,

I remember standing in the line for buying fresh Naan (ددوی)
from the bakery when the winds were blowing,

I remember I was best friends with happiness, shouting with laughter,

I remember the fresh smell after the rain,
as if playing with my best friend, happiness,

I remember never wanting to say goodbye to the heart of Asia,

I remember I carried my beautiful box of memories with me,
I remember my tears writing the story of immigration,
I remember not knowing how much I loved you
until I had to leave you, my homeland.

- NILA SAFI

42

My Homeland

I have become homeless,
I have been moving from one home to another,
I have been in dark waiting for light,
I have died every day
waiting to see you,
without you
I have always been with sorrow,
shoulder to shoulder.

My homeland,
exhausted of persecution, unsung and silent,
My homeland
in an incurable pain.

My homeland,
like two eyes waiting,
My homeland,
like a desert full of dust,
My homeland,
like a grieved heart.

My only love,
when will you get well?
When will we walk together again?
When will you caress me again
with your calm hands?
When will I hear your pleasant laughter again?

When? When?

– Zahra Ahmadi

To My Homeland

Nothing feels better than being in you, my motherland,
enjoying life with my family and my people.
Nothing tastes like the soup, burger and kebab near your streets.
Nothing smells like red and pink flowers in front of the houses.

Nothing is like playing *ladu* with my cousins and joking with each other,
Nothing feels like playing soccer in the streets
with no shoes and two goals made of two rocks.
Nothing has the smell of kabab in front of restaurants,
Nothing feels like a big family sharing the floor, around a tablecloth
decorated with *kabuli palaw, manto, kabab,* and other delicious foods.
Nothing feels like sitting in front of my grandfathers listening to them
talk of when they were young, flying their kites on top of the roofs,
or playing marbles in streets.

Nothing feels like sitting with my family in the garden
with green tea and candies in the afternoon when the sun is going down,
Nothing smells and tastes like the onions, tomato and green paper dancing
in the oil and melting while chicken is joining them
and people waiting to eat *chicken kari* near the street.
Nothing sounds like walking through busy outdoor markets
with sellers singing out what they have and yelling their price
so people will come to them and buy their product.

Nothing feels like dreaming myself back home, enjoying my family meals,
and walking my streets with peace, as if everything is the same as I once knew.

– Ali Siena Ahmadzada

A Love Letter to My Country Central African Republic

I remember the day I left you with pain
crying into your warm hand. Holding my hand
you did not want to let me leave,
but the war made us go far away from you.

I remember the war in your land, how it came to Bangi City,
the war turned your flag into the color of blood
and cut you in pieces.
On one side, war, on the other side, war,
people crying for help, and you trying to hold their hands
and save them from not getting killed,
but not all of the people could take your hand,
I said, "My country let go, let go,"
but you did not hear me,
but I heard your heart talking to me.

Now I remember your bleu ocean that I use to swim in,
every day I would take a ball and throw it into your waves,
your bleu water would laugh back at me
and I would take your fresh sea air inside
and feel your cool water on my body.

I remember your market places, you, my country,
the Central African Republic with your people
moving around, left and right.

Every day I hear you call me home.
   Oh my county,
     Oh my country,
       Oh my country.

- AHAMAT BIRE

LETTER TO MY HOMELAND

Oh, my country, Ethiopia,
you have given us so many chances
that no one has ever given to anyone.
You have carried us all these years
hoping that we become one.

But the hate that we have for each other
still haunts us, like it was just made for us.

Please, let's think about this hatred and war
for those innocent people that are dying
without even knowing their own kind,
without even starting their journey.

– ANAWAR KIMO

To My Beautiful Country, Somalia

My beautiful county, Somalia,
I remember the war in your streets,
I remember when I saw people killing each other
and other people running with their children.

My motherland, I remember all the pain that war cost you,
I remember the children lying in the street bleeding out,
I remember my mother losing her mind,
because my dad died when he was protecting us
from the people holding guns and machetes.
I remember hearing people shouting for help
when the enemy was sexually harassing the mothers and daughters,
I remember the enemies giving guns to the children
to kill their own family and giving them drugs to get high
to do harmful things to people.

My hope for you, Somalia, is that children will never carry guns or do drugs.
I dream of seeing you, my Motherland, peaceful and quiet and beautiful again.

– Yasin Saed

WHAT I MISS

From the moment I left Guatemala
I missed my friends, my pets, my family, my home,
the warmth of the country, the freedom to express an opinion,
the freedom to play, and above all
speaking the language that I respect and appreciate-
Spanish,
The first language I think and learn in,
The first language I speak and read in,
Cuando regrese, I will embrace my dogs,
Cuando regrese, I will reunite and reminisce with my friends,
Cuando regrese, I will thank my family for supporting me when I needed it,
Cuando regrese, I will especially thank my mom
for giving me everything I need and more.
And when I return
I will also thank everyone
who supported me and believed in me.
One day I will return.

– IMANOL ORTIZ

LO QUE EXTRAÑO

Para el momento que deje Guatemala
Extraño a mi amigos, mis mascotas, mi familia, mi hogar
Lo caliente del país, la libertad de opinar,
La libertad de jugar, y sobre todo
Hablar el idioma el cual respeto y aprecio:
El Español,
El primer idioma con el que pensé
El primer idioma con el que aprendí
El primer idioma con el que hable
El primer idioma con el que leí
Cuando regrese voy abrazar a mis perros
Cuando regrese voy a reunirme y hablar con mis amigos
Cuando regrese voy agradecer a mi familia por apoyarme cuando lo necesite
Cuando regrese voy agradecer en especial a mi mama por darme todo y mas
Y cuando regrese voy agradecer igualmente a todos los que me apoyaron y confiaron
en mí.
Algun dia regresare.

– IMANOL ORTIZ

MY HOMELAND OF VIETNAM

I was born in Nha Trang City,
I lived in a house quite near the sea,
I could walk three minutes to the sunrise
to my favorite spot for watching the sea,
the sea view every morning is beautiful with the color of sunlight,
the sky in the morning is blue and orange and sometimes red.

I miss many foods like banh mi
made of noodles, herbs, and meat,
I miss banh mi, the Vietnamese dish of the people
easy to make and delicious,
the bread cut in half filled with pork,
raw vegetables, chili and mayonnaise sauce,
I wish I could eat it every day
and share it with my whole family.

I miss wearing the traditional Vietnamese *ao dai*
white in color, with silk fabric,
Ao Dai is worn by women during our festivals
or to parties, sometimes the dress has colors like flowers,
red or purple, green or black, or any color that is chosen.

When I think of my homeland I miss my grandmother, Bon,
I miss her soft voice telling me stories and answering my questions,
I miss her chicken and her spices,
I miss her kindness,
and I miss my grandmother's beautiful smile.

– UYEN CILL-PAME

LETTER TO MY HOMELAND

I miss you, my homeland you are full of love.
Viet Nam, my country
forever grateful to our heroes.

Vietnam is the green spring,
flowers bloom in four seasons,
the countryside is peaceful,
only hearing the wind blowing
through the ears and the singing of birds.

In the morning, sunlight sparkles,
as warm as sitting by a fire,
the wind helps bring strange flavors to my nose,
coffee smells so strong like a man waking up
early in the morning,
afternoons sitting by the beach.

How peaceful it is to hear the sound
of the sea undulating,
looking up at the sky at night,
the stars are so bright.

– THANH TRAN

Poem to My Homeland

A country whose flag is made of three marvelous colors: Black, Red, & Green,
A country Called Afghanistan,
A country loved by every Afghan,
A country locked by six different countries—Pakistan, Iran, Tajikistan,
Uzbekistan, China, and Turkmenistan,
A country with no access to water,
A country called the Heart of Asia,
A country with 70 percent of its land covered by mountains
With the Hindukush as the highest mountains in Afghanistan.
A country crushed by the superpowers of its time,
A country called the Graveyard of Empires,
A country which suffered the most pain and wars,
A country where my people are starving,
A country with every tear that drops down from the hearts
of my people hoping for peace,
A country we dream of rebuilding,
A country which is still alive and continuing to live,
A country which is still breathing and wants to rise up.

– Haroon Halimzai

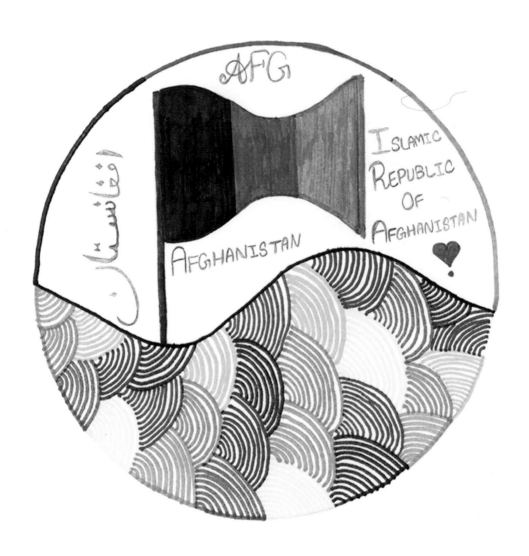

To My Country, Afghanistan

I remember the three colors of the Afghani flag,
Black, Red, and Green,
I remember the sounds of barking dogs and the singing
of birds that woke us up every day, every morning.

I remember the screaming of my people
wanting peace,
I remember the people who sacrificed their family, their legs, their hands,
and even their eyes in war.

I remember saying goodbye to the cold water of snow in the river,
I remember saying goodbye to the people who do not have homes,
who are living in the mountains, not in buildings,
sleeping on the land, not in beds,
drinking from their hands, not in a glass.

My country, I can still see the students working on a road,
in place of drinking tea in a café,

I can still feel the smell that comes from the clothes
and the walls of my home.

– Shahab (Shahabbudin Naizi)

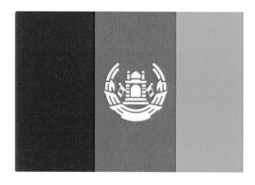

Remembering My Country Afghanistan

I remember the broken windows of my destroyed school
where we were studying in the morning,

I remember the people who lived on a road
looking for shelter to spend their nights in safety and in peace,

I remember the children who needed to go to school in a district
with a lack of schools,

I remember those families who live in slums in Kabul,

I remember the families who are starving to death waiting for someone
to give them food to eat and spend their day with enough to stay alive,

I remember the people who were trying to run away
from my country because of war,

But I also I remember the smell of *biryani* in the evening, a smell that spread
throughout the house and made me hungry,
and I remember the dark, thick woods surrounding me through branches,
I remember the red roses blooming in spring spreading their smell like perfume
and the broken pumpkins, growing in flat dark brown soil.

I remember the long blue rivers with running water
and the raw roads being cracked by the walking of thousands of feet
and the driving of hundreds of cars.

I remember the flowers growing up in the window and the trees in the forests,
and I remember my Afghan people sharing happiness
and sorrow with each other.

- Khyalddin Niazi

55

I Miss My Homeland, the Marshall Islands

I miss my people in my homeland, my family who are still there
and my loved ones who are no longer alive,

I miss the streets of the islands with their cracks that no one repairs,

I miss my friend Meriam who always helped me
who always shared her stories of her life and struggles,

I miss the one small elementary school in my town
that did not have enough books or supplies for the students,

I miss my little town with only one dry goods store and one bus stop,

I miss the women with their patience when they could not find enough
food for their families,

I remember the wars of yelling and fighting and too much drinking
among my neighbors,

I remember the families who waited for someone to feed them,

I remember the woman who needed help and how we neighbors
brought food and clothes for her family's hunger,

I remember the children who did not have a way to make their dreams happen,

I remember all of the sadness and poverty in my small place, Rairok
which looks at the bay in my island country
where the seas are rising.

– Alicianna Subillie

Letter to My Country, Eritrea

I miss the green leaves around my wall,
I miss the wind in the night when it hit my face
 while I was sleeping on my bed in the yard,
I miss the colors of the trees in our yard,
 the Guava, Mandarin Orange, Grapes, and Lemon trees.

I miss my friends Thabt, Fares, Fatohi, and Zidane,
I miss my aunt Najat and my uncles Abdulgader, Akram,
Haj, Abdoljalel, Khaled, and Muktar,
I miss playing soccer with my friend Faris in the sand of our neighborhood.

I miss my grandmother's voice waking me every morning in the dark
to pray and read Quran, a voice that sounds like it comes from heaven,
when I hear my grandmother's voice, I feel comfort in my heart,
her hands are like a warm cloth touching my head,
her words reach my heart like a sharp arrow,
I miss watching her hands putting the *berbere* in the *sherow*,
I miss her face of sunshine, full of feeling and care.

– Anes Mohammad

Letter to My Country

A land that is covered in sand,
A land where the women dress in bright colored dresses
of orange and red and greens, and wear necklaces
and earrings made of gold, silver and beads.
A land of stone houses that are white as swan feathers,
and as white as white flowers.

– Fatouma Abdi

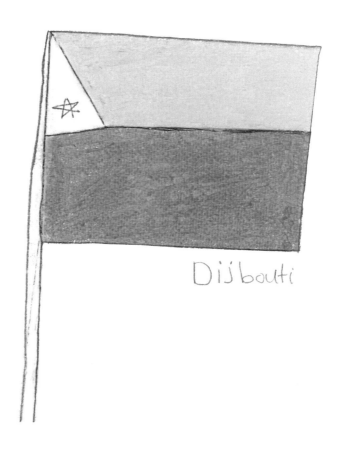

Djibouti

A Love Letter for My Homeland, Somalia

My homeland, Somalia, you gave me the warm tea with milk,
the hot weather and the blue ocean.

You gave me every morning with my mom waking me up for school.
I miss when I used to sit outside with my family and have tea with them.
My homeland Somalia, I will always keep you in my heart.

My homeland, I will never forget the time
when people were dying, when I was a young child.
Somalia, I dream that someday the war will stop once and for all.

– Keyrun Osman

A Love Letter To My Homeland

I remember my place at 7:00 in the morning, with young girls wearing hijab
with long dresses to go to *dugsi* and start learning the words of Allah.

I miss the smells of anjera made of teff flour, salt, yeast, water
and goat livers cooked with oil, onions and jumbo,
and the tea spicy with cardamom, cinnamon stick,
and ginger, served with camel milk.

I remember saying goodbye to my sisters Ilhan and Ayan
and my brother Ilyas and their young children Shukri, Rayan,
Mahamed, Abdalla, and Haawo luul while they were crying.
I remember my heart felt like an empty box.

When I left my beautiful Mogadishu, I knew I would miss the sounds
 of the fresh air when the raindrops fell and the good satisfying smell of it,
I knew I would miss the sounds of my neighbors
calling their children, *Warya, Warya,* yelling for them to come home.

When I left my house in Mogadishu, I knew I would miss the sounds
of the animals, chickens, goats and cows,
I knew I would miss the loud singing of the waves of the ocean.

The day I left, I remember that I struggled, I was alone
traveling from Somalia, to Kenya, to the U.S.

When I left my house in Mogadishu, I believed one day
I would return to my Motherland.

– Hafso Sheikoma

To My Lovely Country, Thailand

I miss your old, hot village district called Ban-Nong-Poung,
I miss your long dirt road beside a huge farm,
I miss your red hot campfires in a cold windy winter when I used to cook
a golden *Khaojee*, grilled sticky rice in the early morning.

I miss your black large buffalo
and a huge white Ox with two cowsheds beside your house.

I miss my old blue bicycle that stayed with me for a long time,
 "You are part of my family!"

I miss your one skinny sour Tamarind tree that was placed in an unknown farm,
a farm with no fence or boundary where I could walk on its land
take what I wanted, and no one would care.
I miss that old Tamarind tree that I used to climb up
in hot weather to be a roof for me.

I miss my auntie คุณน้า *náa* Cee, I miss her cooking,
I miss how my grandfather คุณตา '*dtaa Dit* would prepare the rice
early mornings before school.

I miss my auntie Cee pushing her cart on the village road full of the meatballs
she buys every morning when she rides her motorcycle to the market by herself
and returns with a huge bag of different kinds of meatballs called *Lug-chine*.

I miss those times in my village when I took a bucket and made a drum,
and my friend pushed me with my drum in a cart on our village roads
and friends followed and danced, and I played the music in my head,
I miss that music, those friends and those times in my village.

– Phubodin Nacharoen

62

A Love Letter for My Home and Mango Tree

When I left you, my village, I knew I would miss the sounds of the open air,
the sound of people who spoke the same beautiful language as me,
the sound of roaming around wherever I pleased without fear.

I remember saying goodbye to my bamboo home that was built
with silky, strong bamboo by the villagers that were closest to my mother.
I remember our house standing strong with mango and orange trees
full of bright orange orbs hanging up and dancing like puppets.

I remember saying goodbye to my family's mango tree
planted by my father before he moved to Malaysia,
even when small, the mangoes were sweet
like a hive of wild honey.

I miss the smells of sweet and sour mangoes
from the many mango trees near my bamboo house.

- Lili

LETTER OF THANKS TO MY HOMELAND

I want to say thank you to my hometown, Ho Chi Minh City,
the city of my birth,
the city of my childhood,
the city of my unforgettable memories.

I want to thank the people who sacrificed their lives
to fight for the country,
I want to thank the unsung heroes of the wars
who devoted their entire lives to the country,
who are not honored as those in high-ranking positions,
who are unknown to anyone including me,
for them, I offer my gratitude.

I want to thank the leaders who led people on the right path
to become the beautiful country Vietnam is now,
a country with the world's largest cave, Son Doong,
a country with beautiful beaches and mountains
and rock formations coming out of the sea,
a country where the beauty of traditional dress
the *ao dai* fills our streets with silk colors.

I want to thank my teachers in the martial arts class in my country
who taught me many lessons in life,
by overcoming their own struggles,
I learned to overcome mine.

- HOANG PHAT NGUYEN

64

Letter to Burma

The day I left I remember the landscape,
green grass, leaves falling from trees,
the homeland, the town, was once looking good to me,
everything looking great.

Now the citizens are suffering
under the military coup control,
hot air in the daylight, citizens protesting for freedom
wishing to get help from other countries.
Cold air in the night, fresh air that made them feel relieved.
Now it's all about surviving from the evil military,
burning houses at night.
My country, Myanmar needs help.

Now I miss the smell of the fresh air,
now there is smoke, fire and gun shooting,
and you my Motherland say to me,
This isn't a place where we need to be fighting,
Let us encourage each other, let us fight for our rights,
Let us not kill ourselves, like shooting birds in the sky.

As I was forced to travel from my country, the trees changed
from each place I traveled,
place to place changed, first to a house in the country,
then to a house in the city, after so long
the city where I arrived was in Malaysia.

The moment I reached the city, I entered straight onto a bridge,
I saw buses, I felt like I lost my head in the middle of the night,
the light of the city sparkling, the colors of the night,
people walking into the stores, eating, working, cooking,
I was hearing different languages. I told myself,
it was what I expected, how different people create
who they are by where they are,
and I told myself
I would always miss my village and my homeland.

– Suan D. Pau

What Brings Us Together
Poems of Family and Friendships
Homeland Kitchens
and Shared Meals

Words from Our Poets

~ We can really think we are back in our countries when we are writing our poems. If you start thinking about your old memories the deep words will definitely come from the bottom of your heart. Poems are a way to never forget your culture, your language, your food, your family and your homeland when you are an immigrant.

~ Poems help me connect with classmates who understand the loss after leaving my hometown, memories that never fade are always in my heart.

~ We are living in the same world, but we are separated through borders and cultures. Poetry is a source to remove those borders and connect us through our hearts. Poetry can hold and bring us together.

ODKAC

I remember the smells and sounds
coming from my mother's kitchen,
the food my mother prepared
sambusa, chicken *biryani*, and *odkac*.

I eat and remember my mom
sharing family stories
as she mixed flour with salt
and beef steak with *xawaash*
and cardamom powder,
she spoke of what my grandparents went through
and how hard it was to live
without food and shelter
losing families and relatives
in front of their own eyes.

As she sliced tomatoes, chopped onions,
cut carrots, and minced garlic,
her eyes welled up from
memory and onion
as she recalled how war was in front of them.

Cooking brings out the stories we need
to learn from, as if mixing spice with stories
folds together our life and emotions,
and sharing food together
helps us share life together.

My mother's kitchen is a safe space
to talk about war and death,
to talk about the meaning of sacrifice
and not giving up,
over a full plate of *odkac*.

– HAFSO SHEIKOMAR

*Odkac is a Somali dish consisting of preserved meat.

Letter to My Grandma

To my beautiful grandma, I give this poem.
I remember your big bright house,
The house full of flowers, trees,
Lemon, guava, papaya, pomegranate, and *Rihane*,
The house of my childhood memories,
The house where I was once lost in its rooms.
I remember the injera you were making,
I miss your beautiful sound in the early morning reading Quran,
I miss the stories of your childhood you were telling me.

Thank You grandma for teaching me respect,
Thank you for your kindness,
I am where I am because of you.

I will come back to your house, my house,
To see your beautiful eyes,
To hear your amazing stories,
To eat the delicious food you cook,
To listen to your voice that sounds like morning songs,
Thank you grandma, thank you!
بسام

– Bessam Mohammad

CHANGING MOON, THE SPIRIT OF MY GRANDMOTHER

I am a 17-year-old boy from Saigon, Vietnam,
I left in 2019 when my moon was 70 years old,
I left Vietnam not knowing if it was the last time
I would see my moon,
would others take care of my moon as I had?

I know the moon,
I know the moon is still bright,
though she is filled with loneliness.

The moon knows that life's not easy,
so she doesn't want me to worry about her.
But even the moon is hard to trust
because this life is not easy.
I know the moon does not shine as she pretends to,
I always give the fake smile under the moon
hoping my message will fly to the sky
to let her know the truth,
that I am not happy in the new land.

And I miss her waxing and waning,
I miss her moving across the sky, always visible to me,
but I must lie to her that I am good and show her that I am carefree,
and I know from our last video call, that she is not good.

I know one day I will not see my moon,
she will pass into my memories of loving and loneliness,
my light in the darkness, gone forever.

And I have to be stronger every day without her light,
I will never forget the brightness she gave me,
when I no longer see her guiding me, a dark time will come,
but no worry *Ba ngoai*, I will be stronger than yesterday,
please trust me, *con yeu ba…*

–MINH TRI NGUYEN

Love Letter to My Mother

Your eyes, calm as leaves in the forest,
Your eyes that sparkle when I am sorrowful.
Your eyes are seeing through me. Your eyes, soft, gentle.

Your heart, with mine always. Your heart, loving those who love you,
Your heart forgiving me, your heart, staying happy forever.

Your voice, soothing my fears,
Your voice, praising me,
Your voice, calming me,
Your voice, helping me through tough times.

I remember the smell of spicy curry from your kitchen,
I can see you when I close my eyes,
You are too far away.

From your ever loving daughter.

- Sharmila Nur Islam

FOR MY FAMILY IN BURMA

This is for my father, my baba, who is in Burma, suffering,
my baba who is old and cannot hear well,
in my country that does not care for the old or the young.

It is for the lack of money in my country,
for the lack of medical care,
for the lack of lifesaving vaccinations,
it is for my country where my people
old and young suffer and die,
because of no medical care,
because of war and shooting.

This poem is for my Rohingya Muslim people
forced to hide, who cannot find peace anywhere,
who must hide everyday in the jungle from the guns
of the military ready to shoot.

It is for the sadness of my family,
for the sadness of my father,
for the heartbreak of my mother,
for my little brothers and sisters,
how can I send them money?

This poem is for their fear hiding in Bangladesh,
where harmful people come at night and burn
their fragile hiding places,
burn shelters, take clothing and food
from the people who are already poor
lacking food and clean water,
cooking with outdoor fires,
living in flimsy shelters that do not protect them
from rain or flood, danger or soldiers.

It is for those in America, who do not see our struggle,
I speak out against selfishness when my people are suffering,
I speak out against those who turn away.

– SHARMILA NUR ISLAM

A Love Letter to Aunty Ele

I miss the loud joyful sounds coming from you,

I miss all the laughter in my home because of you,

I miss your stopping by and giving us sweet tropical Hawaiian candy,

I miss the smile on your face like a sunny day,

I remember the pain I had when you left, like my heart just broke down,

I remember you bringing my dad Samoan food like corn beef and *wahoo*,

I remember the phone calls of your beautiful voice like a blue ocean,

I remember the beautiful times we spent together talking and laughing
with my siblings,

I miss the look in your eyes like a dark blue night,

I remember not getting to see you in your casket because of Covid,

I miss not seeing you every day, like a shooting star in the sky,
you are gone.

– Losivale (Losi) Palaita

FOR MY UNCLE

My uncle, my hero, was born in Somalia, Sakow,
my Uncle, my mother's brother
took me in as his son, wiped the tears from my face.

My Uncle is my namesake,
he is patient, strong, and helpful.
He is by my side, when something is wrong
he encourages me to do the right thing
and helps me solve my problems.

My uncle loves to go to the Mosque,
he loves to pray to God,
he doesn't pretend about his religion
or his beliefs as a Muslim.
To me, he is the angel that God sent to earth.

I remember his room,
simple, a single bed,
a prayer mat where he used to pray
five times a day from the Quran,
the holy book of my religion.

My uncle, my hero.

- YASIN SAED

THE SHARED MEAL

A shiny kitchen invites me,
I step in on my soft wool slippers
Towards the waving smells,
Everyone waiting for a bite,
Dreaming of the tastes to come.
My mother stirring the skimmer
So the okras won't split,
And let those sticky seeds flow into the pan.
Chopping cucumbers, adding to شوملی/ توروی
With mint leaves swimming in the glass,
And leaving us hungry.
Our famous Afghani food منتو
Made with love and passion,
Kneading the dough until smooth,
Spreading, spinning, rolling,
The spices mixing up together
And the hissing sound of Pepsi pouring,
Gathering as a family on the floor
Nothing but caring and sharing.
The divine evening becomes more beautiful,
The bitter taste becomes sweeter
As we witness the togetherness
And lift up our hands for *dua*.
الحمدلله, الحمدلله , الحمدلله

- KALSOOM MEHRABB NIAZI

76

GAMBIAN MORNINGS

My favorite Gambian food is *Tiga gaya sombi*
peanut and rice porridge.
Tiga gaya sombi is a Soninke breakfast
our great- great grandparents used to eat it
Tiga gaya sombi.

It is heavy and warm,
a morning meal I love to eat,
it keeps me full and gives me energy
throughout the day,
energy for completing my assignments
and my other work.

Most days my mother cooks *Tiga gaya sombi*
for the family. When the sun is waking up
she drums the mortar and pestle to pound
the ground nuts before blending the raw rice and peanuts,
then she pours cool cups of water into her cooking pot
and she lets it boil,
next, she puts the mix of peanut and rice
into the hot water, and cooks and stirs
the soft rice and peanuts bubbling in the pot.

Finally, when it's done,
she adds sugar and milk
to give it that sweet taste.
My family loves *Tiga gaya sombi*
a gift from our ancestors.

– MOHAMED LAMIN CEESAY

My Father's Pho

Oh, it's great to have a hot bowl of pho in cold weather,
when my dad cooks pho on weekends,
I often drive him to the market
to buy ingredients and help him cook.

For a good pot of pho we use beef,
beef bone, rare meatballs and tendon.
A complete bowl of pho must also have star anise,
cinnamon, scallions, coriander and herbs.
The herbs and spices create the fragrant broth,
we put the herbs in a bag, tie it closed with string
then peacefully place it in the stew pot with beef bones.

My father stews it for 2 or 3 hours to let the bone juices out.
Oh, it's great to have a hot bowl of pho in cold weather,
the smell of pho makes me feel at home.

When my father cooks pho for everyone to eat,
I want to say thank you to my parents and to Vietnam
for letting me enjoy this nourishing meal
that has traveled overseas, like me
to feed people from other countries.
Thank you, for making me proud
that I am Vietnamese with a bowl of pho.

– Hoang Phat Nguyen

Poem in My Father's Voice

I am strong,
I was born with fear
in a dark world full of tears and bloodshed.
I am a strong man who raised 9 children
during war in Cambodia
when people were dying every day.
I am a leader who keeps people safe
by hiding them in secret places.
I am a strong man who runs away from violence
while trying to find food to feed my family.
I am a man who hid in a big farm
with a small pot and smaller fire
to cook the rice and fan the smoke
flying to the sky,
scared of those who would see it
and come.

I am proud of what I have been through,
I am a man
who is trying to move away
from those painful memories,
I am a strong man.

– Husni Asmat

FOOD OF MY DREAMS

Rain was coming down like heavy rocks,
outside the sky was like a dark cemetery,
suddenly, I smelled the spices coming together,
Mom was crushing and cutting the onions
putting them into the double boiler,
the tears in her eyes running down
like the rain outside.
Rice was expanding in the pot,
chicken was dancing, ready to run into the double boiler,
Mom was putting the masala on,
making the fascinating smell of *Biryani*
fill the house and our hearts.
Who could hold themselves back to eat this *Biryani*?
Can't hold back to eat her *Biryanii*.
Can't hold back.

- HAROON HALIMZAI

TALKING WITH MUZAMEL MUWAHED, ONE OF MY BEST FRIENDS

Haroon's note: The lines in italics are Muzamel's

I am from the landlocked country in the heart of Asia, Afghanistan.
I, too, am from this beautiful mountain country called Afghanistan.
I am from art and love. I am from my mother and my father.
I am from books and articles about Nature and environment.
I am not jealous of what comes before me.
*I am from a family who always respect each other by loving them,
and accepting whatever elders say.*
I am the tree which is planted by a river and can't be removed.
I am a cook who brings up the very oldest and traditional food.
I am grateful for everything that I have.

- HAROON HALIMZAI

Remembering My Best Friend

I remember my friend, Shabnam, my best friend,
My friend who rises like a sun,
My friend who turns boring lessons into fun,
My friend who made me live every moment of my life.

My friend who led me to the beautiful truth,
A truth that makes me love the world and myself,
My friend who flies me through the purple skies of friendship,
My friend that I never wanted to say goodbye to,
My friend that I never wanted to lose.

But, I lost my friend between strangers,
I lost my friend between wars,
I lost my friend between the sound of bombs and hopelessness,
I lost my friend between rules and traditions.

My friend, I miss her more than before,
My friend, my eyes are looking for her more than before,
My friend, my tears are looking for her more than before,
My friend, my heart is saying "PLEASE COME BACK" more than before,
My friend, I never wanted to say goodbye to,
My friend, I never wanted to lose.

– Ada Safi

My Time

Ada's note: This is a conversation between me and my cousins. I am talking about how I grew up. And my cousins, Shikab Safi and Muhammad Safi, are talking about their best childhood memories. Their words are in italics.

I am from a kingdom that has no limits, Afghanistan,
I am from a clever king and a benevolent queen who honor me like a princess.

I can't forget those days of mine in a playground with my friends - a life full of joy,
I can't forget the first bicycle of mine, which my papa bought with love, not money.

I am from flying through the blue skies of Kunar
with nothing but freedom in front of me.

I remember being a king and finding treasures in my home,
treasures that answer my deepest problems.

My family raised me with love,
not with money.

I still remember smiling at my childhood,
my memories are the only things from my childhood I could keep.

I am from the gifts my family gave me, faith and attitude,
a faith that holds every human together,
an attitude that withholds cruelty and spreads kindness.
I am from the gifts my family gave me, traditions and rules,
a tradition that dresses you with royalty,
rules that protect you from suffering,
I am a person of free mind,
I am a person of free will.

– Ada Safi

محدویت نلری، زه د هغه سلطنت ځخه یم چی ۸ هیڅ

زه د یو هوښیار پاچا او مهربانه ملکي څخه یم چی ما ته د
شهزادگی په ټیر درناوی کوي.

زه نشم کولی زما هغه ورځي له خپلو ملګرو سره د لوبی په ډګر کي هیري کرم - له خوښنیو ډک ژوند
زه نشم کولی خپل لومړی بایسکل هیر کرم، چی زما پلار په مینه اخیستی و، نه په پیسو

زه د کنر په نیلي اسمان کي پرواز کوم چی زما په مخ کي له ازادی پرته بل څه نشته.

زما په یاد دي چی یو پاچا وم او په خپل کور کي خزانی پیدا کوم
هغه خزاني چی زما ژوري ستونزي خُوابوي.

زما کورنی زه په مینه لوی کرم
نه په پیسو.

زه اوس هم د خپل ماشومتوب موسکا یادوم
زما یادونه زما د ماشومتوب څخه یوازینی شیان دي چی زه یي ساتلی شم.

زه د هغو ډالیو څخه یم چی زما کورنی ماته راکړي، باور او چلند
داسي عقیده چی هر انسان سره یوخای کوي
داسي چلند چی ظلم لري او مهربانی خپروي
زه د هغو ډالیو څخه یم چی زما کورنی ماته راکړي، دودونه او قواعد
یو دود چی تاسو د شاهیت سره جامي کوي
هغه قواعد چی تاسو د رنځ څخه ساتي
زه یو ازاد ذهن انجلی یم
زه د آزادي ارادي انجلی یم.

The Taste of Happiness

Here I am where life put me,
how I miss my old man's food,
I want to try that flavor again, but it's not time yet.

Where I was born, my mother raised me with a bowl of beans.
My father taught me to enjoy the flavors of beans and eggs however humble.
I loved eating Mom and Dad's food, no matter how often it was in the week.
I loved the taste of tacos, although he was rarely able to buy them.
I remember his voice calling my brothers and me to eat together.

The memory of a table with little food, but many shared smiles,
The memory of that exquisite smell of Mama's food,
The memory of her face, her eyes of happiness when seeing that once again
Dad was able to bring money so that we children could eat delicious as always.
They taught me that what is cooked with love, is unsurpassed in flavor.

- Perla Del Rosario Garcia Moro

Ode to My Mother Tongue

Spanish, I write this to thank you for everything you have given me.
Thank you for giving me the opportunity to talk of you.
Thank you for giving me the opportunity to think of you.
Thank you for giving me the opportunity to read about you.
Thank you for giving me the opportunity to learn from you.
Thank you for giving me the opportunity to see you,
And thank you for giving me the opportunity to write about you.
- Imanol Ortiz

Oda a Mi Lengua Materna

Español, te escribo esto para decirte gracias por todo lo que me diste.
Gracias por darme la oportunidad de hablarte.
Gracias por darme la oportunidad de pensarte.
Gracias por darme la oportunidad de leerte.
Gracias por darme la oportunidad de aprender de ti.
Gracias por darme la oportunidad de poder verte,
Y gracias por darme la oportunidad de escribirte.

- Imanol Ortiz

LAS DELICIAS CHAPINAS

Dear Guatemala,
I want to thank you for all your *tipica comida*,
But I want to tell you that
Even if I am in other *tierras*
You and your famous delicacies will live in my mind and *cocoro*,
I will never forget the smell of your *raices* when the rain fell,
Your *tomates*, potatoes, and rich *ayotes* that sprouted
From the womb of our mother earth.

I want to thank you for your splendid drinks,
Fresco horchata, jamaica, nance, tamarindo,
For the pure water derived from your peaked mountains,
For these fresh *limonadas en los días soleados*,
For giving me the opportunity to *nacer, crecer y aprender*
Of your wonders of fruits that with great sacrifice
Tus guerreros help to harvest.

Now that I'm in another country, I can only remember
Your flavors, your traditions, your cultures,
Your crazy ways of preparing things
Los tamales, los chuchitos, el pepián, los rellenitos de plátano,
Everybody loves you including me, I really love you!
I swear that I appreciate all the little things *que tu tienes en tu corazón*.

I promise you that one day I will travel again
To your beautiful warm and flowered lands
Because I miss every part of your strong and delicate peaks,
The peaks with which you rejoice in your own beauty.

I devour coffee in the morning on a rainy day
And remember you,
And praise you,
And long for you.

– JENNIFER CAROLINA CARRERA GARRIDO

Mother and Daughter Poem

Zahra's note: My mother's voice is written in italics

I am from the crowded evening sky
full of different colors of kites,
from the sweet and juicy Baklavas,
making me starve for more bites.

*I am one of those Afghan women
that had to give up on her dreams
for a dirty political game,
so, I brought you to the USA
to not experience the same.*

*I am child of a commander
that sacrificed his life to prevent a disaster,
you should always remember
that your grandpa was a brave protector.*

*I am from the Atan on wedding nights
to the outstanding Nawshakh heights
from the bloody war sights
to the worthlessness of human rights.*

I am from a country whose *Anar seeds
are as scarce and special as rubies,
whose mountains are like precious treasures
and whose people can never be separated.

I am a girl with high dreams
who is not afraid of failing
even If I lose my hands and feet,
I will still go after them crawling.

I am an Afghan,
a country whose beautiful face is covered with war,
whose ears are deafened by sounds of bullets,
and whose tongue is dumb with fear.

– Zahra Ahmadi

* Pomegranate seeds

88

THE CROWN JEWEL OF THE TABLE

It's a sweet, not a food,
Its taste is magical,
It is not western-it is eastern,
Its right is always reserved.

Tastes like it did not come from the world,
It is the crown jewel of the tables,
You can't get enough of its walnuts,
Its pistachio is even more wonderful.

Turkey is its original land,
But it's more popular in my homeland,
Its name is registered to us,
People of my country are also in its taste.

Have you guessed what it is?
Of course, it is Baklava.

– ZAHRA AHMADI

THE SECRET

The secret of my healthy and happy childhood
was the food that my grandparents prepared.
The striking sounds of pestles hitting mortar,
crushing garlic and onion,
and the smells of garlic and onion
hitting the oil
were always a part of my childhood.
Wherever we went, we brought something new
for the face of *dastarkhan*.
Walking in the scorching sun
we used to carry impatience within ourselves.
When the door of the house opened
we smelled the smell of tomatoes and green pepper
fighting in the oil.
We all used to run to Bubie, grandma, with the same question,
And Bubie would give us all the same answer,
"Be patient, first go and wash your face and hands."
And looking at those dishes
راچ‌آ, هتلاس, یبمورش, کرکوس, یپلگ, ایبول, هباس
it was as if we found the biggest happiness of our lives,
the red beans cooked well in the bath of tomatoes,
the fresh rainbow salad sprinkled with dry mint,
the smell of hot naan (یدود) which made us feel warm.
After reading the (میحرلا نمحرلا هللا مسب),
waiting for our elders to start eating first,
after taking the first marie (همقل),
marie is much more than a first bite,
it can't be translated,
I can't wait to take the second one,
Ukhhhhhhhhhh
I bit my tongue again with my impatient teeth!
Hahahahahaha
laugh again, grandpa.

– NILA SHAFI

"dastarkhan," a spread of dishes arranged on a tablecloth that might be laid on the floor. You will be provided a cushion to sit cross-legged upon, (having removed your shoes at the door). Guests are usually given an individual bowl or plate, but utensils are not used; meals are eaten with the right hand, using bread as a scoop.
No matter how hard-pressed, the Afghans treat their guests with immense respect and will go to great lengths to serve them the best food possible.

togetherwomenrise.org/customsandcuisine/customs-and-cuisine-of-afghanistan

MEMORIES OF EID

I remember the plates and plates of food
made by my mother with love,
the *biryani* waiting for us on
the colorful *dastarkhan*.

I remember the cardamom smell in *biryani*,
the green pods pounded with her strong hands
the spice of the chicken and rice.

I remember making *qably*
with friends on the first night of Eid
waiting for everyone to come
so we can visit families.

I remember the smell of *kabab*
the garlic and onion grilling
after performing *qurbani* for Eid.

I remember inviting my friends
over to enjoy meals at night
and going to sleep
at my uncle's and aunt's house
a family reunion
all of us staying up late.

I remember this joy spreading everywhere
in our house, with my friends and family
during our Eid celebration.

– KHYALDDIN NIAZI

MARQA

Married women in my country Ethiopia
are the only ones
who can make *marqa*,
a mound of delicious dough
with a hollow center
brimming with butter,
the most beloved dish.

Married women
are the only ones who know how
to perfectly fold the barley flour
and salt and milk together
until it changes to soft dough,
and when it's done
to pour in the butter
so that it wells up in the center.

Married women
know to make this with love
and intention for their family
and the ones they love,
it is a gift given
to enjoy and nourish.

– ANWAR KIMO

92

OUR AFGHANI KITCHEN

Red tomatoes, white potatoes, and green peppers,
smells of cooking anywhere, everywhere in the kitchen,
to call us to eat.
My mom stirring new smells with every meal,
my mom cooking our favorite dish, *Kabuli Palao*,
m own tears flowing
while my mom cuts onions and spicy peppers.

The smell of fresh vegetables
wake me up, like a morning sun,
telling me it's time to come together and sit around دسترخوان,
to bring us to the *dastarkhwan*, a beautiful Afghani cloth,
covered in food prepared by my Mother,
can't wait to take a bite
thanking God for everything
that He gives us, after eating.

– SHAHAB NIAZI

Zigni

Dear America,
I am writing this poem
to introduce you to my Eritrean food,
a beloved spiced dish called *zigni*,
traditional food for Ethiopian and Eritrean cultures,
a blend of berbere with onion, tomato, chicken and boiled egg,
the tomatoes leftover from Italian colonization.

When the vegetables and chicken meet in the pan,
it's like two old friends reuniting after years apart.
When I smell the *zigni* with my grandmother's fresh injera,
I run to her kitchen,
the smell of her *zigni* makes me hungry.

We sit on a mattress on the ground,
we say *bismillah*
by the name of God before we eat,
and we eat with our right hand,
joining the injera with the *zigni*.

After we eat, we thank God for the food,
we say *alhamdulillah*
to indicate the meal is over.

– Anes Mohamed

SAMBUSA

Sambusa,
you taste like my childhood,
you remind me of my culture
and the generations of Somalis before me.
Sambusa,
you are important to me and my family,
my big sister, Amran, makes you when it is Ramadan.
Sambusa,
your spicy meat, red pepper, onions
fried in hot oil
taste like hope.
Sambusa,
you are from my childhood,
your taste makes me remember my childhood
when it is time to break the fast.
Sambusa,
the sound of the boiling oil
is the soothing sound of the ocean waves.

– KEYRUN OSMAN

POEM OF PEACE

To my little brother who I lost when he was only four years old.

I dream you and I are flying
over the peaceful clouds in the sky
wearing a white cloth dancing over
the peaceful wings of a butterfly
and a white bird.

The day that you disappeared flying over
the peaceful place in the sky,
white smoke all around you,
I was calling your name,
Anaheim, Anaheim, Anaheim, Anaheim
wait, wait, wait, let's fly together
in peace and build a new life
in the sky, above the sunshine
and near to God.

— AHAMAT BIRE

the mood light of Poetry

Speaking Out in an Unforgettable Year

Words from Our Poets

~I wrote for those people who want to speak.
All those words that were the tongue of my heart
are called poetries.

~Poetry gives me the right to say what I want to say,
poetry gives me that space that nobody gave me before.

~The difficult things we have now as migrants are that
there are still problems, such as racism or the lack of
English communication and isolation by Americans;
they should be voiced, rather than silenced.

~Poetry can be used to mention the problems of the world
like climate change, injustice and hunger to convey
a strong message to the leaders of the world.

The Poem in the Time of War

God, please help me and my family
get away from this scary world,
from the flow full of blood around the body,
the sound of screaming, the sadness in their voices,
the house with silence and darkness,
the rain and cold with thunder and night.

Because of this war everybody forgets
who they are,
they forget their religion and culture,
all they want is just to survive,
finally, the war ends,
but the scary memories stay stuck on you.

- Husni Zamir Asmat

The Poem in the Time of Conflict

The poem in the time of conflict,
When people struggle around the world,
Some from war and some from hunger,
When strong, big countries try to steal lands.
In the time of conflict, conflicts become part of our life,
The time when our lives depend on a push of a red button.

-Bessam Mohammad بسام

A Poem to Emotions

Moving to the world I always dream of,

Something stopping me to blend in,
in this dream world,

I hear a sound inside me
saying reality is holding me back,

Truth is holding me to not blend in this dark world,

What I always think of as the dream world is actually a world
of lies and more lies.

-Ada Safi

The Poem in the Time of My Brother Going to War

I cry for my brother
please don't be killed by others,
you're the best among brothers
parents love you more than others.
Who is happy in the whole world
to see their children kill people?
Twenty four years of nurturing care,
how can we be calm with killing?
So, I beg you to not die,
the president is not always right,
who are you fighting for
when bright red blood wets your hands?

– Minh Tri Nguyen

Rice in a Time of War

The rice is delivered to the front line,
we're hoping for food from our village,
but not, our village has been razed.
The bowl of rice in my hand comes from the paddy field,
the fragrance of a grain of rice does not end in itself,
nor in the sweat in the field,
but comes from the bones and blood of our compatriots.
Even when a bowl of rice holds all the flavor we love,
we are full with anguish and the bitter taste
of those who have fallen.
We don't know who GI Joe is,
we don't know why we're fighting,
we want only to return home for a peaceful life,
but because our home was destroyed by a B-52 bomber
we turn fury into action, where is my rice bowl in a peaceful village?

– Minh Tri Nguyen

LET TRUE DEMOCRACY BEGIN

Why does my country need to have hatred and pain?
In Burma, recently the military has started a war,
why the suffering? In my opinion the military chief thinks this world is his,
so my people lost their lives to guns.

Many people were gone by the hand of the Burmese soldiers,
but we the Burmese people are not strangers,
we are equal and we do not need any killing,
we do not want powers to control us, our country is waiting
for you, the dictators, to stop this hurtful, painful feeling
that you, the dictators, tolerate
causing us, the Burmese people, to live through
tribulation, sadness and affliction.

We need to return back to our motherland,
she is calling us, like a waterfall,
we want our unhappiness to flow away, let the past be past.

Let our motherland give us hope,
Let our true democracy begin,
Let there be forgiveness.

- SUAN PAU

STOP STARTING A WAR

Stop killing our Afghani people.
Stop making fun of them.
Stop playing with innocent people's blood.
Stop closing schools for our young girls.
Stop taking children away from their mothers.
Stop making oceans from our children's tears.
Stop punishing them for their existence.
Stop taking the sun's light from their harmed faces.
Stop turning the young generation against their country.
Stop giving guns to our young men.
Stop starting a war at the start of everyday.

– KALSOOM MEHRABB NIAZI

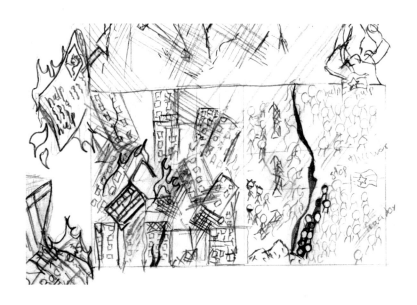

I Am Writing For My Homeland

I am writing for my homeland that was destroyed by the Taliban,
I am writing for a country that has been under attack for almost 40 years,
I am writing for my country where there is no freedom.

I am writing for a country where girls can't go to school,
I am writing for a student who used to go to school with no shoes.

I am writing for a country with no president.
I am writing for a country with no peace.
I am writing for a country with no police.

I am writing for a woman whose son died in her arms,
I am writing for a man whose wife died in front of his eyes
and there was nothing he could do.

I am writing for the people who left everything
except themselves just to get out of their country.

– Shahram Faizi

I Speak for My Homeland

I speak for my homeland, Afghanistan,
I speak for the government to build more
schools for children to study,

I speak for people to start helping each other
by giving them anything they can, give them
clothes, buy them food,

I speak for COVID-19 to stop spreading around
to those who cannot tolerate you, stop killing
people all around the world,

I am writing for my country that has been under
attack for more than 40 years,

I speak for my country to see peace in it,
I speak for the Taliban to stop killing innocent people,
stop closing schools and to allow students to study,
to become someone they dream of in their future,

I speak for my country to see peace in it.

– Shahab Naizi   105

POEM OF I SPEAK

I speak for the mother that lost her child,
I write for the war to stop killing the children,
I write to save them from war
and give them a better future.

I speak for my country destroyed by militants,
our home and our dream lost because of them.

I write for my grandfather and my grandmother
that I never saw them in my life
but I hear their history everyday.

I speak for the bird flying in the air and the forest
to find something or somewhere to land.

I write for the government to save our planet
from the climate change.

I write for my brother that I lost,
I have not seen him since we were young,
I write for his memory
that lives in my head and my heart,
I write for his birthday
that we cannot celebrate together.

– AHAMAT BIRE

POÈME DE JE PARLE

Je parle pour la mère qui a perdu son enfant,
J'écris pour que la guerre arrête de tuer les enfants et sauve,
Eux de qui leur donnent un avenir meilleur.

Je parle pour mon destroyer de pays » par militarts
Notre maison et notre rêve perdus à cause d'eux.
J'écris pour mon grand-père et ma grand-mère que
Je ne les vois jamais de ma vie mais j'entends leur histoire
Tous les jours.

Je parle pour l'oiseau qui vole dans l'air et la forêt
Pour trouver quelque chose ou un endroit où atterrir.
J'écris pour que le gouvernement sauve notre planète
Du changement climatique.

J'écris pour mon frère que je dure,
Le voir quand nous sommes jeunes,
J'écris pour sa mémoire qui est
tête et coeur,
J'écris pour son anniversaire que nous
Je ne pouvais pas célébrer ensemble.

– AHAMAT BIRE

Now Is the Time

Now is the time to change the world
because it is never too late to stop a war,

Now is time to stop hurting our motherlands
and our children,

Now is the time to give children their dreams,

Now is the time to forget the gloomy clouds,

Now is the time to listen to our mother earth
who is crying out for us because we create fighting
and make the skies dark with war.

– Lili

What I Want

I want people to care for each other,
I want people to be safe,
I want people to stop killing each other,
I want the oceans to be clean so animals can stay alive,
I want people to respect their parents,
I want people to end wars.

– Fatouma Abdi

THE POEM IN THE TIME OF COVID

The time when people of the world are locked in their houses,
The time when people are dying because of the virus,
The time when people can't be together,
The time when all people need to stay six feet away
from each other.
The time when we can feel afraid to go outside,
The time when we are on our phones feeling like no one cares
about our health,
The time when we worry
if we go outside to exercise, we might get arrested.

– ANES MOHAMMAD

THE POEM IN THE TIME OF COVID

The poem in the time of Covid
from the poison virus outside the circle,
Covid penetrates
deeply into people
causing those who are still alive to cry non-stop
for those who have died.

– THANH TRAN

POEM IN THE TIME OF COVID-19

The poem in the time of Covid-19,
isolation, worry, sadness, depression, illness, pain,
suffering, and death, in one word, tragic
like the waves of the sea forming a whirlwind,
painful as a stab in the heart of a brave person.

The poem in the time of Covid-19,
an inopportune time to stop classes,
a direct pass to the world of antisocial meetings,
a bad time to say "stop," you must stay away from me,
episodes of food shortages,
more psychologists receiving patients
due to increased isolation.

The poem in the time of Covid-19,
we've had social distancing meetings,
social distancing races, social distancing hugs,
social distancing talks,
communities suffering, many evicted from their homes,
families suffering from hunger
because they cannot carry their daily bread,
children isolated, coughing from polluted air,
attached for hours to their screens.

The poem in the time of Covid-19,
do not lose faith that one day
this hateful microbe will leave our planet.
Someday, will these years, 2020, 2021, and 2022
become a bad memory?

Might there come times of peace and tranquility?
Might we come together for food, for love, for peace?
Yes, to a world that changes.

— JENIFER CAROLINA CARRERA GARRIDO

For My People

I speak for my country, Afghanistan, to the pain
of children who no longer have food to eat,
I speak for the people of my country who need food, jobs and peace,
I speak for my country when women and girls come out to the street
and call for help! and help!
I speak for the people in my country who worked to build the country
in the past 20 years, but then everything changed again like the past,
and it was destroyed once again.
I speak for my feelings and my hope for my country,
I speak for homeless, poor, sick, and disabled people,
I speak for my family that helps me and provides me what I need,
I speak for my religion; I will not forget where I came from,
I will never lose or leave my religion.
I speak for all youth who have big dreams,
I speak for returning to my country to help rebuild,
I speak for those who cannot say what is in their heart,
and for those who have lost their family.
I speak for those who served their country and their people,
I speak for those youth who need financial aid and scholarships
for their education,
And, I speak for myself to work hard
and chase my dreams and make all these things happen.

– Ali Ahmadzada

DREAMING OF RIGHTS FOR EVERYONE

I grew up seeing peoples' voices buried under the ground.

I dream of a world fair for all people,
especially the ones that are in a dark place.

I have hopes for all the Africans that are in the hell of Libya
to be saved and have an opportunity to live a life again
by the holy blue God.

I have seen the world's shadow part, so I am thankful
for my life being in the world's bright part.

I dream and I hope for everyone to have civil rights.

– TIEDA TSEGAY ARAYA

FOR THE WOMEN

I speak for the women who one day left the house
and stayed in the pockets of people with hearts of stone
and heads of paper,

I speak for all the girls and women
who face internal suffering due to a bad love affair,

Today, I write for all the girls who are brutally hurt
internally and externally, when their innocence hangs
on a fragile thread from the days of their birth.
I speak for that flower that was cut without permission,
I speak and I scream for all those little angels
whose wings were cut by denying them
permission to fly.

I speak for those who are sold like oil,
like goods, like real estate on the internet,
their empty faces on the stage, on the anvil of the night.
Were they not raped, were their bellies not filled with lead?

I speak for each young woman or girl
who wanted her freedom,
who wanted to be free,
who wanted to live entirely in freedom,
free from a world full of wounds
where every day they stumbled
and were flooded with fear.

I speak for myself and for all the fragile girls,
fragile, but fighters,
sentimental, but sincere,
hurt, but strong,
where in too many corners of the world
they are enclosed in four walls.

I speak with the hope that the waves of the sea
will return them whole
from where they fought and were broken.

– JENNIFER CAROLINA CARRERA GARRIDO

I Speak for the People of My Country Afghanistan

I speak for the women in poverty in my country who are sitting next to *naanwaie*,
the bakery, in their blue chadors hoping for just a piece of naan,

I speak for those children who are collecting plastics
from the side of the road to warm their houses,

I speak for those girls who are not allowed to have an education
because of their gender,

I speak for the old men who sit at the side of the road waiting and waiting
each day in the hope of finding work to bring a piece of bread home,

I speak for those who cannot see their loved ones again,
the ones who never had the chance to say goodbye,
whose loved ones disappeared from bombs or violence on the streets,

I speak for those mothers who are sitting next to the hospital door hoping
for what the doctor will say, longing to hear the words, "don't worry, don't worry,
your child is fine, not hurt in bomb blast,"

I speak for those people in my country who have no one
to ask them if they are alright,

I speak for those who do not believe in humanity anymore
because of today's reality,

And I speak for those who are still hoping for a better tomorrow.

– Nila Safi

I Will Speak

I will speak for my country Somalia,
I will speak for my Somali people who are losing their homes
because of climate change,
I will speak for the animals who are in danger because of climate change.

I will speak against the president, because he is killing
his own people,
I will speak for the children in my homeland
who are needing food and water, who are without homes,
I will speak for the people who are living with hunger
who lack rainfall, their dry fields filled with war.

And I will speak for the powerful mother to lie down and rest,
And I will speak for the grandparents to stay under the big tree house
and have a honeymoon.

– Keyrun Osman

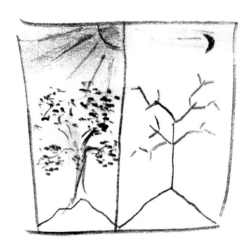

POEM OF I SPEAK

I speak for my country, The Gambia, that I will never forget,
I speak for my grandfather Mohamed who is very sick, may he recover well,
I write for my cousin Baba who I miss since leaving my homeland.

I write for a ferry I always crossed in Janjanbureh when traveling
to the village Diabugu to visit my grandparents,
I write for my brother, my mother's first born son, who died
when he was three months old.

I write about people cutting down trees in my homeland.

I speak for the election that happened in my homeland,
I speak against the current president who lost, yet refused to step down
for the winning president and now sends his army
to be killing people on the roads.

I speak for myself and my family who were forced to move
to the village for a month when the *ECOWAS people came for the president
and took him out of the country
and people started coming back to their homes.

I speak for my former school in my homeland, a great school
with teachers, the principal and staff members who I respected
who respected me.

I speak for the day in the USA, for the tragic fire that happened
in New York on January 9, 2022, around 11 am,
I write with sorrow for the 19 people from my homeland The Gambia
who lost their lives because of the choking smoke and fire.

I speak for my country The Gambia that I will never forget,
I pray for my country to have peace.

– MOHAMED LAMIN CEESAY

*The ECOWAS (Economic Community of West African States) is an ongoing military intervention
in The Gambia by several West African countries. The intervention was launched to resolve a
constitutional crisis caused by a disputed presidential election. (Wikipedia)

118

FOR THE THOUSANDS OF REFUGEES AND MIGRANTS DETAINED IN LIBYA

I speak for the people that are in the hellish countryside of Libya,
who most people alive don't even know they exist,
whose voices are buried not in the fresh earth,
but their flesh is buried in bloody mud, their screams
to the deaf world can't even break the barrier.

I speak for the people who are in the Sahara, the empty, vacant desert,
that are looking and screaming to find someone,
it is like they are lost in a dream of a house of darkness
and they cannot see anything,
a dream from which we can wake up, but they are stuck
in the dry, deserted place, the dry desert, without hope.

I speak for the father who must lock his own tears inside
his heart, knowing if his tears joined those of his wife
their weeping would not stop, leaving the children
in too much sorrow.

I speak for the mother who hit her heart like drums,
making the floor of her house into an ocean
of countless tears.

- TIEDA TSEGAY ARAYA

119

For My People in Burma

I speak for what I believe in.

I speak for my Burmese people destroyed by the military
meant to protect us from harms,
but instead became our enemy.

I speak for the earth destroyed by people fighting each other
because of jealousy and greed for more money and more lands.

I speak for families who lose their loved ones because of wars and the pandemic.

I speak for my people in Burma,
whose houses were burned down
by the Burmese military,
who must now hide in the forest.

I speak for my people in hiding,
I speak for their safety,
for their lack of food and water and shelter.

I speak for human rights in all 57 countries where
people do not have the right to do what they want,
to dream of their future.

I speak for children in Burma, North Korea and all countries
where they lack food and dreams,
and cannot go to school because of poverty.

I speak for my Burmese people, that they find their freedom,
that they can walk in their own peaceful land
without fear or hiding in the forest.

– LiLi

I Write for My Homeland

I write for my homeland El Salvador, where in the past
the government caused the country to fall into violence and trouble,
I write against my country's government that stole the peoples' money.

I write for the new president who is trying to change my country's history,
who is trying to make my homeland a better place for my people.

I write for the people that suffered in the past,
I write because the rules are changing
for the people that harmed others
for their own benefits, the ones who let people down.

I write for my people to let them know we are with them
and we will never give up.

– Luis Orellana Mendoza

I am the voice of the people who are forced to leave their homes
because of climate change,
I am the place where 7 billion humans live.

I am not the one who pollutes the air,
I am the one dealing with polluted air and increasing CO2 causing coral reefs to die.

I am not Miami Beach carrying danger being near to water than can flood me,
I am suffering from heat since the industrial revolution started.

I am not the one who causes people to live in loneliness,
I am not the place which is being destroyed by the creatures called humans,
I am not the one who causes darkness in people's hearts,
I am the one who brings joy into people's hearts.

I am not the garbage that people leave behind
or the floods that destroy homes,
I am the shining blue sea
with tall coconut trees
and little restaurants on the road.

I am not the giant factories polluting the air,
I am not the wild fires burning the green lands,
I am not the peace that is slowly disappearing in the world,
I am the beautiful river of Kunar د کونړ سین which shows the honesty
of the people who live there.

I am not deforestation,
I am the beautiful pink flowering spring tree
which tells us it's time to relive life one more time.

I am not the military plane who comes down and burns buildings and houses,
I am not the person making the world worse,
I am not a gun shooting animals for sport,
I am not a tree chopped down to make more houses when we don't need more,
I am the curiosity that wonders around the world,
I am the clouds up in the air that observe the world,
I am the blue sky that flows around the world.

I am not climate change making the earth heat up,
I am not the sufferer of fear and worry outside the window,
I am the sun bringing the light for the earth,
and the quiet river moving through the trees.

I am not the rain bringing flooding to the plains in Vietnam
making many people lose their houses,
I am the ocean that brings the rains to life
for the plants and the forest.

I am the blue ocean waves that dance in the sunlight,
I am the ocean that sharks, dolphins, octopus and starfish live in,
I am ocean beaches where people swim and play on a sunny afternoon,
I am the powerful crocodile inside the water,
I am the black dangerous tiger in the forest,
And I am the garden with healthy soil and vegetables.

I am not the volcano that destroys the homes of the animals,
I am not the gunshots of the war that kills people,
I am not the war that destroys people's lives and homes,
I am not the disaster that cannot stop floods going to each nation causing damages
destroying homes and lands.
I am not the climate change that hurts the earth and tears it apart,
I am not the oil spill that kills the beautiful sea animals in the oceans,
I am not the war that brings fire.

I am the strong mountains giving shelter
to animals that lost homes because of climate change,
I am the strong wind that blows away the war and fire,
I am the Mekong river of Vietnam flowing with the moonlight,
I am the shy panda living safely in the mountains of China,
and I am the purple lavender whose scent brings peace.

— Collaborative Poem by the Stories of Arrival Poets

NATURE POEM

Nature, I can hear your tears calling and yelling
in the middle of the night, calling for help,
but they cannot hear you,
their minds focus on taking over
countries and planning wars.
They cut your trees with no hesitation,
they no longer know the meaning
of beauty.

– MUSTAF OSMAN

CLIMATE CHANGE

Spring breeze no longer smells of sweet flowers,
everything is out-of-season and smells of garbage,
February's warm rays are no longer safe,
the sea is still the sea, but rising more than last year,
the old pirate game and the glass bottle
now replaced with plastic bottles and plastic bags.
The starry sky where many wishes were raised in the past
now it's blank from urban lights.
Blue sky is replaced by the gray of smoke,
vast forests only on TV,
wild beasts only in memory,
facing resource depletion,
facing the change of all species,
facing the change of the earth,
facing human self-destruction.
What should we do?

- MINH TRI NGUYEN

Gió xuân không còn thoảng mùi hoa ngọt
Mọi thứ thay bằng sự trái mùa và rác thải
Tia nắng ấm tháng 2 không còn an toàn
**Biển vẫn là biển nhưng sâu hơn năm trước
Trò chơi cướp biển và chai thuỷ tinh khi xưa
Giờ thay bằng chai nhựa và bao ni lông
Bầu trời sao nơi bao nguyên ước được cất lên khi xưa
Giờ là một màu đen và ánh đèn đô thị
Bầu trời xanh thay bằng màu xám của khói
Những cánh rừng bạt ngàn chỉ có trên tv
Những con thú hoang chỉ còn trong kí ức
Đối mặt với sự cạn kiệt nguồn tài nguyên
Đối mặt với sự thay đổi của muôn loài
Đối mặt với sự biển đổi của trái đất
Đối mặt với sự tự huỷ của con người
Chúng ta nên làm gì?

- MINH TRI NGUYEN

POEM: A TRUE STORY

The ocean is like a carpet for the planet protecting it from harm,
trees help the planet, making it green and beautiful
like a new grown flower,
the birds are like clouds flying above the blue wide sky hoping to land somewhere
where green grass ends.

Some people still plant their dreams in the ground
watering them, hoping for the seeds to grow roots
and their plants to reach the clouds.

But, in our time of struggle, suffering from a virus and climate change,
when governments say they will do something about it,
instead they build what is causing climate change
and waste millions in building factories
that pollute the air and rivers,
tell me, why don't they donate the money
to thousands of people without a home, suffering
from hunger and thirst, with torn clothes?
                Please,
tell me how we can come together
and make the world a place
where there are no wars and hatred,
a world where we live in harmony,
where we come together.

– MUSTAF OSMAN

For Samoa, the Environment and the People

I write for Samoa's protection,
I speak for the sea levels rising in Samoa,
I write for homes destroyed by terrible storms.

I write for my Samoan dad who has cancer and is fighting strong,
I write for Samoa with high sea levels changing the land.

I speak for our ocean filled with trash and plastic bottles,
I write for the sea animals choking on the garbage,
I speak for the air we breathe filling our lungs,
I write to solve climate change
to give Samoa a shield of protection.

I write to speak against wars and shooting around the world.

I write for the pandemic to end and leave us alone with peace.

-Losivale (Losi) Palaita

FOR ALL, FOR THE EARTH

I speak for my country Afghanistan suffering from injustice,
I speak for my country's people living in poverty,
I speak for all people living with hunger,
I speak for all the lives lost from Covid 19,
I speak for our planet's pollution,
I speak for the danger of rising temperatures, heating our planet
beyond survival,
I speak for coral reefs dying from warming seas,
I speak for coastal communities flooding from rising sea levels,
I speak out to industries making climate change irreversible,
I speak out to those who tell others climate change is a hoax,
I speak for all the scientists trying their best to wake us,
to show us that climate change is happening right now!

- KALSOOM MEHRABB NIAZI

Poem, I Speak For

I speak for my homeland Somalia
where my people are desperately poor and are facing a drought.

I speak for the homeless suffering from hunger and thirst.

I speak for the earth facing climate change.

I speak for making the sea become clean as the blue sky,
and the air fresh as a cold glass of water.

I speak for the time when we stop cutting trees
and bow to their beauty in the forest.

I speak for listening to the trees telling us to stop.

I speak for the end to violence,
I speak for people to come together and solve the problems
of violence and crime, of people shooting and killing each other.

I speak for the time when we will stop judging other races,
I speak for the time when racism will end
and we will honor all people.

I speak for all of us to come together in peace.

– Mustaf Osman

Now is the Time:
A Prayer for My Country

Now is the time to pray the five daily prayers and ask Allah for peace
with all your heart, to give *sadaqah* to poor people, and go to *Hajj*.

Now is the time to grow beautiful flowers, *jaalo* and *cadaan*.

Now is the time for everyone to get work, not judging the tribe they are from.

Now is the time for children to wake up in the morning
and head to school to learn about the beautiful world.

Now is the time to build hospitals in places where pregnant mothers are dying
because of the long distance to travel for doctors, or nurses and safe care.

Now is the time to build libraries for impoverished parents
who are worried about their children's future life and their education.

Now is the time to listen to our hearts and follow our dreams.

– Hafso Sheikoma

A Poem In the Time Of

A poem in the time of my happiness,
A poem in the time of my dreams,
A poem in the time of my imagination,
A poem in the time of my good days.
And a poem in the time of my unforgettable memories,
A poem in the time of bad things happening all around me and my people,
A poem in the time I am scared of losing the ones I love,
A poem in the time of my darkness and sadness,
A poem in the time of leaving my country, Afghanistan,
A poem in the time of missing everything and everybody in my country.

– Shahram Faizi

WHAT I WANT

I want everyone to feel free,
I want people in my country, Cambodia, to have food to eat,
I want the world to have peace.
I want my friends to have jobs in my country,
I want the people I love to have a better life,
I want my family to be rich,
I want the world to be peaceful for poor people.
And, I want to wake up from a place that is shining
and feels fresh like I'm on top of a mountain
where I can see all of nature, the plants and animals,
and hear birds singing with the sound of small rain pouring,
and from there I can smell my grandmother's curry from a nearby kitchen,
what I want from these smells and sights and sounds
is the feeling that I am far away and by myself.

- HUSNI ZAMIR ASM

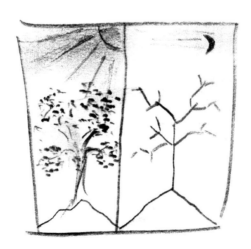

Now is the Time

Now is the time to talk to fish to understand how to live more peacefully,
Now is the time to understand why the tree is so beautiful
and wonder how high it can grow,
Now is the time to speak with friends to learn about how they live,
Now is the time to return to 2019, because at that time
my grandmother was still alive for me to give her a hug.
Now is the time to look at the sky, clouds, sunlight and rainbows
to let go of all sadness and sorrow so your body relaxes.
Now is the time to look up at the starry sky to touch your dreams,
Now is the time to blend in with the pure white snowflakes
to let yourself drift.

– Thanh Tran

Now Is the Time

Now is the time to pray for staying well from Covid
to be healthy and safe,
Now is the time to set the table for hope,
to fill our glasses with love,
Now is the time to dance in colorful clothes
to swing our arms to the rhythm,
Now is the time to spend time with family,
to talk to each other and to laugh together.

– Fatouma Abdi

Now Is the Time

Now is the time to look at the twilight and dream of the peace of sunrise,
Now is the time the wind gazes at the leaves,
Now is the time the wind blows and gathers the trees
and casts a lonely shadow,
Now is the time the wind is hissing and the cold wind blows,
Now is the time for the warmth of the sun and the trees,
Now is the time to return back to our motherland,
She is calling us, like a waterfall.

– Suan D. Pau

CHANGING MYSELF

Now is the time to change myself
because now I feel there is only one color
that makes me paler and makes my life tasteless.

If I change myself
by learning new things on my own,
researching next steps by myself
it will make me feel more diverse
and colorful like a rainbow.

Now is the time to take care of my family
and spend more time with them.
Now is the time to know
what I have gained,
to make me into my many colored dreams.

- HOANG PHAT NGUYEN

KEEPING A FLAME

I speak for my homeland Vietnam,
I speak for my village Tien Giang,
I speak for the orphans who have died, forever in everyone's heart,
I speak for the climate change in Vietnam, polluted by smog,
I speak for everyone to protect the environment with its fresh air
and beautiful landscape.
I speak for everyone that you keep a flame
of your dream inside of you, do not extinguish it.

- THANH TRAN

THE PERFECT WORLD

A world where there is peace and calm,
A world where everyone has a dream,
A world where our dreams become real,
A world where no one suffers from hunger,
A world where there aren't any borders,
A world where our planet is green and clean.

– BESSAM MOHAMMAD بسام

Afterword

By John Fox

The Voice of My Heart bursts with energy, with inspired and heartbreaking words and artwork by refugee and immigrant students. I believe that our world (and I mean each of us alive in the world) needs these particular voices like we need water, food and air.

These *Stories of Arrival* poets, guided by the remarkable team of project founder and poet, Merna Ann Hecht, and Multilingual Learner classroom teacher, Carrie Stradley, are arriving with a profound and unique perspective. Each young person brings with them experiences that too often are unspeakable. Yet, their poems speak to us when we read of their journeys of forced flight from their native country. If not literally forced flight, there are still the very hard decisions made by parents and family to leave one's home ground based on profoundly stressful factors.

Reading these poems allows us to learn how each person is making their way – with courage, resilience and authenticity. If you want these qualities in your life, then don't miss reading *The Voice of My Heart*. For most of us, there is a lot to learn about migration, displacement and creating a new home in a new land. These poems and poets, if given the chance, are superb teachers.

The Institute for Poetic Medicine, has acted as a funding partner of *Stories of Arrival* over ten years, and we are deeply proud of and grateful for this work. Your purchase and enjoyment of *The Voice of My Heart* helps complete this circle of sharing and your support and interest sends out expanding, concentric circles of the truth and hope this book brings.

Truth and hope that is living, that is a life-force, from these poets who are the voices of the future.

John Fox
Founder, CEO, The Institute for Poetic Medicine

Acknowledgements

Words of immense appreciation go to community members, colleagues, friends, family and organizations who provide our project with generous financial backing and with encouragement, partnership and abiding friendship that honors our mission of bringing refugee and immigrant youth voices into the center of community life.

Thank you to Shahrzad Shams and John Fox for their eloquent words in the foreword and afterword. Throughout our years of affiliation with the Institute for Poetic Medicine, John has been a source of guiding wisdom and camaraderie of the highest order. IPM's commitment to bringing the life-enhancing language of poetry to diverse community settings has helped sustain the years of our work. We are honored that we are an IPM Poetry Partner Project and grateful to John and the IPM board members for consecutive years of funding.

The production of this book is owed in large part to financial support from the amazing board of the Tukwila Children's Foundation. Their commitment to the wellbeing and full potential of Tukwila children and youth extends to our project and enables it to thrive. Mayor Ekberg, Kate Kruller and the entire city council, Tracy Gallaway and the Tukwila Arts Commission and Charis Hnin of Talitha Consults all add to the welcome that the young people who make Tukwila their new home receive. We also thank the Tukwila School District Board Members; Foster High School Principal, James Blanton; Assistant Principals, Clint Long and LaTanya Parker; SPED Educational Support staff member Rachel Lavender and teachers and cultural liaisons who add their support to our project. Special thanks to Instructional Technology Specialist, Theren Hayes, for his assistance in helping create a podcast website for recordings of student poems.

Our community support extends to a partnership with the King County Library System (KCLS). Tukwila Teen Services Librarian, Gregory Summers, and KCLS Teen Services Librarians, Jaqueline Lockwood and Rebecca Hershey have given many hours of their time and expertise to sponsoring system wide poetry readings and book launches on behalf of our poetry project. We also thank KCLS Program Assistant Christen Lowrey and we extend our gratitude to Rachel McDonald, KCLS Teen Services Coordinator, for her wonderful support of the young people in our project.

We are thrilled to have established a partnership with Kara Martin, Program Director for Tukwila's Spice Bridge Food Innovation Network Global to

Local Program and Faizah Shukru, Food Innovation Network Program Coordinator. Their warm welcome to our poetry project is multifaceted including exhibition space for student created poetry and art, a venue for our book launch and poetry readings, pop-up book sales and opportunities for students from the project to participate in summer meal planning for youth and in community work involving developing monthly arts and poetry events that will feature local youth.

It is my distinct pleasure to work in tandem with graphic designer Richard Rogers whose superb artistic sensibility, extraordinary devotion to this project and expansive generosity bring this book to life. Photographer David Lynch takes photos of each young person for every year of our project with a keen eye and open heart toward creating each portrait. Graphic artist Jenna Riggs has designed the collaborative poems for the second consecutive year and we treasure her innovative design style. We also thank Bruce Rutledge of Chin Music Press, our publisher again this year.

Individual donors make our project possible and we thank each one of you for your largesse. The space is limited for listing everyone who donates to the Stories of Arrival Project though we do want to mention Judy Pigott and Ron Lamb for their bountiful support.

We thank former Seattle Youth Poet Laureate Wei-Wei Lee and local and internationally known Hip Hop artist and community activist King Khazm for their zoom presentations. We are grateful to WA State Poet Laureate, Rena Priest, also a zoom guest of honor, for her inspiring writing prompts and her powerful poems. Thank you to cellist Michelle Dodson for her mesmerizing in person performance.

Our gratitude goes to ninth grader Suan D. Pau who designed the front and back book covers, equally, we thank all of the students who contributed the original drawings and paintings that appear throughout the book.

Finally, I extend my deepest thanks to project co-director Carrie Stradley who has welcomed me into her Multilingual Learner classroom for every year of the Stories of Arrival Poetry Project. She is a gifted educator who transforms her classroom into a safe, open-hearted space where every student feels treasured and respected. Carrie's understanding of the lives of her multilingual students and her belief in their abilities to succeed remains with them long after they leave her class. Our partnership has provided the conditions for the shared sustenance of poetry to take hold and flourish.

Merna Ann Hecht

MEET OUR POETS

Ada Safi was born in Afghanistan in a beautiful village, Kunar. She is fifteen years old. She speaks four languages: Pashto, Dari, Hindi and English. Her family came to America on September 26, 2019. Her hope is to become the best version of herself. Her dream is to build schools and hospitals in her country. She is thankful for the life she is having where she can do whatever she wants. Ada likes reading books, playing video games and hanging out with her friends.

She who remembers climbing trees in her kingdom of no rules.

Ahamat Bire Dana Soweyman was born in the Central African Republic. He lived in a refugee camp for seven years in Chad. He moved to the U.S. when he was eighteen years old in 2019. He speaks and understands French, Arabic, Sango, Hindi and English. In the refugee camp before he came to the U.S. people were killing each other like animals. They were killing each other like this because they wanted to have all of the power over the country. There were other people who escaped from war who hoped for a peaceful place who wanted to live in peace with their families. Ahamat's dream is to help people suffering from war

to bring them to a peaceful place. He wishes for all people to reach their dreams and have what they desire. He also dreams of bringing his mother from the dark into the light and he dreams of going back to his country and starting a new life of peace.

He who remembers his shining country and who will always miss his little brother.

Ali Siena Ahmadzada is sixteen years old. He is from Kabul, Afghanistan. He lived in Kabul for fourteen years. He came to America on January 10, 2019. He is a junior and he likes to play soccer. His favorite thing to do in his free time is to watch and play and practice soccer. Ali's favorite colors are blue and white. He is a respectful, humble and helpful person for his family and other people. His dream is to become a pro soccer player. His favorite places to visit are Dubai, France, Istanbul, Las Vegas, New York and Hawaii and to return to his country, Afghanistan. He wants to travel the world when he gets the chance. He is always there for people who need help and support.

He who wants to take the Afghanistan team to the World Cup for the first time.

142

Aliciana Subillie is eighteen years old. She was born in the Marshall Islands and arrived in the U.S. in 2019. She speaks Marshallese and English. Her goal is to become a nurse and help people back in her homeland where more medical care is needed. She likes to take care of her home with cleaning and with cooking including traditional food from the Marshall Islands like fish and rice and pumpkin rolls. She is thankful for her family who are very supportive to her. Aliciana joined the poetry project with only two weeks remaining; she created a poem about her homeland and joined in all of the project activities.

She who is from the small place of Rairok, 4,763 miles away from Tukwila.

Anawar Kadir Kimo is fifteen years old. He was born in Ethiopia in a small city called Itaya. He came to the U.S. in 2019 with his siblings. Anwar means "bright;" he was named after someone who used to live with his family. He speaks Oromo and Amharic. Anawar believes in himself and he wants to become a soccer player and he loves seeing his favorite soccer player. He is proud to have a huge family.

He who loves his mother's traditional food from his homeland.

Anes Mohammad Ali is a junior. He was born in his Kingdom, Eritrea. His lived in his Kingdom for nine years and then he moved to Sudan where he lived for four years. He speaks four languages, they are: Arabic, Tigré, Tigrinya, English (and a little ASL). He is a soccer player and he is also a boxer like his grandpa, Mohammed Ali, Jr. He came to the U.S. in 2019. When he arrived, his English was so bad, but he made friends and learned English. He is also good at playing games and he is a good dancer. His name means the person when you sit to next them, you feel comfortable.

He who listens to his elders and follows the rules.

Ayat Bakour was born in the Syrian city of Raqqa. She is eighteen years old. Because of the war in Syria, Ayat left her country at the age of eight. She lived in a camp on the border of Syria and Turkey. Then she entered Turkey after six months to live in a Turkish refugee camp for five years before coming to the U.S. in 2015. She speaks Arabic, Turkish and English. She wants to become a doctor and go back to the country she misses so much so she can help others. Ayat joined the poetry project with only a week remaining; she jumped right into the project creating a poem and joining in the activities.

She who longs to return to her homeland.

Bessam Mahmoud Mohammad is seventeen years old. He was born in Eritrea in a small town called Keren. He is one of six and the oldest boy in his big family. He lived in Sudan for four years before he came to the United States of America in 2019. He speaks Tigré and Arabic and a little bit of English. His dream is to be a doctor or a police officer. He loves poems and soccer. When he feels bored, he listens to Arabic poems. He loves poems very, very, very much, not every poem, but Arabic poems. He has a beautiful, long name, Bessam Mahmoud Mohammad Mohammad Ali. His name means a smile and it spells in Arabic like this: ابتسامة

He who sits in class super calm like Batman in the dark night.

Fatouma Abdi is from Djibouti. She came to the U.S. when she was young. She came with her sister, brother, mom and grandma. She came here to go to school and she wants to be a doctor to help people. She speaks English and Somali. Fatouma is learning to drive a car. Every weekend she likes making black tea in the mornings. And every day she puts green oil, like olive oil on her hair which she likes to do. She wants to travel when she grows up and she would like to see Los Angeles and Los Vegas. Also, Fatouma likes basketball. She works at a grocery store in Tukwila and from this job she helps support her family and she is saving money for herself for college.

She who is proud that she is from Djibouti.

Hafso Abdirizaq Sheikomar was born in Kenya but she is Somali. She has lived in three countries-Kenya, Uganda and Somalia. She speaks English, Swahili and Somali. She lived in Uganda for five years and graduated middle school there. She moved to the U.S with her mother and brother in 2020. She dreams of seeing peace in her motherland hoping that people will stop fighting each other and stop killing innocent people. She also dreams of becoming a nurse and helping young children who are sick. She loves to help people because at one time in Uganda she saw young kids who didn't have any family asking for help while they were bleeding and crying and people were passing by them without stopping to help.

She who dreams of seeing her motherland in peace.

Haroon Halimzai is seventeen years old. He was born in 2004 in Afghanistan's capital city Kabul. His mother tongue language is Pashto and he can also speak two more languages, Persian (Dari) and English. He came to the U.S. on the 20th of March, 2020.Haroon is a hard working person who dreams of becoming a dentist. He is writing poetry too, but he says he is not a poet though he loves to write and to read poetry. He is lucky for a good education and good security because of moving to the U.S. Haroon always prays and dreams of peace for his country so he can move back. He will never forget where he came from and who he is. He frequently writes poetry to express his feelings about his country, about this world, and about the bad situation in his country. Last but not the least, is Haroon's hope for peace and equality in the whole world.

He who always tries to be safe and he who helps make peace.

Hoang Phat Nguyen was born in Vietnam, his name is Phat and his middle name is Hoang. But, when he moved to the U.S., he took his identity papers and chose the name Hoang Phat, and that's why his name is Hoang. He lived in Vietnam for 18 years and he moved to the U.S. in 2019. He arrived with his family in hopes of a better life and future. He knows martial arts and he believes it can help calm him down. Hoang is a person who is said to be a bit sensitive in initial conversations, because when he meets new people he is a quiet person. He does not initiate conversations because he is afraid that

his words might cause others to judge or evaluate him. He is a guy who is often alone, but when he was in 10th grade, he found a new world for himself in martial arts. He made new friends in the martial arts class. They made him feel at home so he considered them as his second family. In that martial arts class, there were many colors to wear and everyone had different stories. This helped him learn many valuable things in his life before he came to the U.S. Hoang speaks Vietnamese and English.

He whose mind is calmed with practicing martial arts.

Husni Zamir Asmat is seventeen years old. He was born in Cambodia in a small village called Angkor Ban. He came to the U.S. in 2018. He speaks three languages, Khmer, Cham and a little English. His dream is to become an ice skater and his goal is to perform in front of many people. His name means "goodness" and "he who always helps his friends and is fun to be around and likes to make people smile." Husni is thankful for his grandparents who took care of him when he was a little boy and who were always loving to him. He likes to play in the garden with butterflies flying around. He hopes to

become a great person who can help people who struggle in life.

He who misses the flowers blooming in the morning when the sunlight shines through the mango tree.

Isaac A Padilla is in tenth grade. He is from Mexico, Sonora. His name means "laughter." Isaac likes to try anything new, different and adventurous. He speaks Spanish and English.

He who loves his Mexico, but doesn't want to go back because it is too dangerous with cartels fighting for territory.

Jenifer Carolina Carrera Garrido is nineteen years old. She was born in Guatemala City, July 13, 2002. She arrived in the United States on May 15, 2019, having left Guatemala on April 30 of the same year. Her native language is Spanish and when she arrived in the United States she had to learn the second language (English) which has been difficult, but not impossible. She is pursuing one of her dreams which is to be a nurse, after which she would like to continue studying medicine but specializing in pediatrics. She wants to learn more than two languages. So far, she does not know what other language she would like to study, but she wants to be trilingual. One of her goals for this year is to be able to serve God in some way and to be able to surpass herself. One of the people who inspires her to move forward is her mom. She wants her mom to be proud of her. When she was around 14 years old, she was nominated as the best GPA girl in school and won first place in a storytelling contest.

She who never stops falling in love with the words that come out of her heart. "Soy Latina."

Kalsoom Mehrabb Naizi is fifteen years old. She was born in Afghanistan. She came to the U.S. on February 17, 2021. She speaks four languages fluently—Pashto, English, Dari, Urdu and a little bit of German. She loves reading books and playing badminton. She likes to cook for her family. She is a Muslim girl and she is proud of her religion and her country. Kalsoom wants to travel the world and she dreams of becoming a doctor and helping other people. She hopes to visit her country and meet her beloved family. She loves her family very much. She will never forget where she came from. Her name means "our prophet's daughter's name."

She who can feel the pain of other people.

Keyrun Mohamed Osman was born in Somalia, but she moved to Kenya and lived there for seven years in the Kakuma Refugee camp. She speaks Somali and English. Before she came to America, she dreamt that life was going to be luxurious, but when she arrived here, she realized that life was hard in the U.S. Keyrun dreams of becoming a doctor so she can help people who are suffering and sick. She misses her friend Aisha and others in Kenya. She wishes she could to go back and give them a big hug. When she came to the USA she was not happy because she had to leave her

friends and grandparents. Keyrun takes care of her cousin Aisha who has the same name as her friend in Kenya. Keyrun misses her grandmother Fatuma, and her big sister Amran who is still in Somalia. She hopes her country will become a peaceful place and she wishes she could go and help her people in Somalia now.

She who misses the blue ocean of Somalia.

Khyalddin Niazi is nineteen years old. He was born in Afghanistan in a small city called Puli Khumr (Dari: پل خمری).   He arrived in the U.S. in February, 2021. He speaks Pashto and a little English. He hopes to become a good software engineer and his goal is to help others, especially his family.

He who remembers the mountains of his homeland.

LiLi, age 15, was born in a village in Chin state in Burma. She lived in Burma for 6 years before moving to Malaysia in 2012. LiLi's father moved to Malaysia first to make money for her family because in Burma people are really poor. There were not enough hospitals, stores, cars, or internet. Because of this, her family and villagers had to walk miles and miles to get to their farms. It was not easy walking because it was muddy and there were leeches that caused the people walking to bleed when they walked for almost one whole day to go to their farms. When LiLi and her family

came to Malaysia, it was because her father insisted. Her mother didn't want to leave her homeland, but people forced Li Li's mother to go. Her mother agreed to leave for Malaysia only because of her four children. She wanted them to have a good education and better life. When LiLi, her mother, her siblings and others who had to leave Burma arrived in Malaysia, it had been a harrowing journey. They had to hide from police and soldiers and on the way they had to walk with bare feet. When they ran, they only ran at night time, so that it was more difficult for the police and soldiers to see them as they escaped.

She who wants Burma to stop warring, to stop harming her motherland.

Losivale Palaita (Losi) was born in Nevada. She is 14 years old. She speaks English, but understands her family's Samoan language. She misses all the fun that she had with her Samoan nieces, nephews and cousins in Nevada. When she first moved to Washington she thought it was going to be like her home. But the weather was so different from Nevada because it was always sunny and hot there, but Washington was rainy and windy. Losi dreams of becoming a pro at volleyball, her favorite sport because she grew up playing volleyball only. She is a shy person when it comes to new schools and

speaking in front of the class. She misses her aunty who passed. Her aunty would always make her and her siblings laugh and was always there for them and her dad. Losi hopes to find a job to make enough money to take care of her family.

She who has her grandma's hair like the wing of a blackbird.

Luis Fernando Orellana Mendoza, grade 11, is from El Salvador. He speaks Spanish. Luis came to the U.S. in 2017 with his brother. He was thirteen when he arrived. He came to the U.S. to have a better future and to make his parents proud of him because they have given him everything they have. Luis likes to play sports and be in nature. He draws strength from his grandparents.

He who travels as far as a river and never stops.

Minh Tri Nguyen (Tri) was born in Saigon City, Vietnam. He lived in Vietnam for 15 years until 2013 when he moved to Seattle with his lovely family. Tri speaks Vietnamese and he is learning English and he is trying to learn another language too. He likes math and physics because he feels good learning them and he has won two gold medal awards in both of them. His name from the Bible means "smart, intelligent, and wise when asking God for good advice."

He who can lead you to a world of abstraction, because equations and numbers are his only true loves.

Mohamed Lamin Ceesay was born in The Gambia. He came to America when he was 6 years old, then he returned to The Gambia when he was 8. He lived in The Gambia for nine years and came back to America a short time ago, in October of 2021. He was raised in The Gambia with his parents. He speaks two different languages, English and Soninke. The language he likes to speak is Soninke because it shows who he is. He understands life better through this language. Mohamed has learned about life through the advice of his elders. He wants to continue in school and get an education. His goal is to graduate from school and attend college to earn a degree in business and try to benefit his mother by providing for her. His dream is to bring peace to his country which is suffering because of crime. He wants to become a good person and to help everyone.

He who wants to give support to young ones, because he also got support from his elders.

150

Mustaf Mohamed Osman was born in Somalia. He came to the USA when he was eleven years old. He and his family came to the USA for safety because they were from a place where people were killing each other and stealing money from each other. They lived in a refugee camp in Kenya called Kakuma, for seven years. The camp was not safe. In Kakuma, thieves didn't care if it was daylight, they would still steal anything they could including cooking pots and pans, clothes and other things. Mustaf hopes he can go back to the Kakuma refugee camp and help other refugees. He hopes to

bring peace to that camp and hopes to stop the fighting. Mustaf has always dreamed of bringing peace to the world. He dreams of graduating one day and becoming a successful person. He misses his friends back in Kakuma and he misses the large, wide field where the people played soccer.

He who sees himself as a ghost traveling around the world learning new things, seeing new places.

Nila Safi, grade 11, was born in Kunar, Afghanistan and came to the USA on September 24, 2019. She came with her family for a better education and started high school as a freshman. Nila's name means "Blue River" which was given to her by mistake while on her way to the U.S. Her real name is Nida which means "unique message" and was given to her by her grandfather. Nila speaks four languages: Pashto, Dari, Urdu, Hindi and she is still learning English. She learned Pashto and Dari which are the official languages of Afghanistan in school and from her family. But, she learned Urdu

and Hindi by watching Hindi and Pakistani dramas, cartoons and movies. Nila has 9 members in her family including herself. The person who inspires her the most is her grandfather. She loves learning and exploring new things. Her biggest accomplishments after coming to the U.S. were being part of Girls Who Could Sisterhood Change Makers, completing the Youth Food Justice program in the summer of 2021 and passing her ELL classes. Nila loves talking to new people and learning about their country, culture, and food. Her dream is to study hard and become a good cardiologist (heart doctor) and help people. She also loves to cook and wants to open a big kitchen in her country which will serve free, delicious Afghani food for all people.

She who speaks like the sound of rain after sadness.

Perla Del Rosario Garcia Moro, was born in Talpa de Allende, Jalisco, Mexico. She lived in Talpa de Allende for fourteen years and then moved to Seattle, Washington in the year 2017. She is eighteen years old and is a senior. She loves to dance. It is her passion. At the moment, she does not practice dance, but since she was a child she was born with the love of dancing. It has always been her dream to be a professional dancer. She misses Mexico because her dad lives there and she wants to go back one day and visit him. She is a girl with big dreams. She dreams one day to give the best to her parents and to help many people financially. She hates lying, cheating and envious people.

She who likes to feel alive and express what she loves with movement.

Phubodin Nacharoen, is a senior. He was born in Thailand in a small town called Prathai, in a village district of Ban-Nong-Puong. Phubodin moved to the U.S. on September 6, 2016 when he was twelve years old. He speaks three languages, Thai, Laotian and English. His dream is to become a mechanic and travel to any country he wishes to visit. He hopes that his future takes the right path and fulfills his plans.

He who remembers the farm full of rice growing in a hot village forest in Thailand.

Sergio Imanol Velasquez Ortiz is fifteen years old. He was born in Guatemala City. He prefers his middle name, Imanol. He speaks three languages, Spanish, Jeirgonza and English. Imanol arrived in the USA on December 12, 2020 at 10:30pm. Like the name "Emanuel," Imanol means "God is with us." Imanol hopes to win a scholarship for college. He dreams of being one of the top students of 9th grade. He also has a goal of being a varsity player for two sports he likes—football and soccer. Imanol was the student with the highest grade in his school in 2014, 2015 and 2016, an accomplishment he is proud of. He is also proud of the support he receives from people who don't know him. He is inspired by his mother, uncle and aunt and wants to be the

best he can be to make them proud of him. Although he likes to play football, what he likes more is talking with his friends in Guatemala. Imanol joined the poetry project with only two weeks remaining. He created several bi-lingual poems and joined in all of the project activities.

He who is in love with his Spanish language.

Shahram Faizi was born in Kabul, Afghanistan. He is seventeen years old. He was born in 2004, January 20. He can speak, read and write in 3 languages—Pashto, Dari and English. Shahram moved from Kabul to the U.S. in 2017, when he was only fourteen. His hope is that he wants his homeland to be free. He knows that his people want freedom. It's been forty years that his country is under attack. People are getting killed every day. He doesn't know the meaning of his name; his mother chose it for him and he likes it. Shahram loves playing soccer. He practices two or three days a week so he can get better at playing. He is thankful

for his family, friends, and loved ones. He loves them all so much. His grandfather once told him, "Do what you love and never give up." Shahram likes spending time learning things. His goal for his future is to be successful.

He whose face explains hundreds of different feelings. He who remembers selling chickens to buy himself a pen.

Shahabbudin (Shahab) Niazi, is eighteen years old. He was born in Afghanistan. He speaks Pashto, Dari, English and a little Urdu. He came to the U.S. on 17 February, 2021. He wants to work for Microsoft and his dream is to have a lot of money. He believes that today in the world you can buy anything you want with money. He loves to have cars and he loves Afghanistan, the place where he was born. He always hopes peace will come to Afghanistan.

He whose skin color is like a leaf of summer, whose eyes are like a tiger.

Shamshidah Nur Islam (Sharmila) is from Burma. Her name means "shiny and happy." She speaks Rohingya, Hindi, and Malaysian. She was born in 2004 and came to the USA in November of 2016. Sharmila wants to finish high school with good grades. She is thankful for her parents and knows that her mother always gives her courage. She has received a medal for gymnastics and she loves to dance and to cook. She hopes that everyone in her country will stop fighting.

She who is missing the smell of Jasmine flowers in Burma, and the smell of spicy curry from her mother's kitchen.

Suan D. Pau was born in Burma. Suan is the second youngest in his family. His family joined his father in Malaysia when he was only five years old. It was in Malaysia that they met their father for the first time. Meeting his father was like a dream that came true. Their father had stayed in Malaysia for about 10 years driving a truck to support the family. After three years in Malaysia, the family arrived in the U.S. in 2016. They came to the U.S. to have a better life and education. Suan can speak Tedim and English, but he used to speak two other Burmese languages - the traditional languages of his father and mother. Now, Suan can't speak those languages since moving to the U.S. He is a Christian and he is proud of it. He is also proud of his ability to draw. Suan's dream is to become a software engineer. His life experiences are helping him build endurance. Graduating from high school and making money is his only hope. He does not believe in so many things, but he knows something important - he knows that if he tries hard to become what he wants to, his dreams will come true. Suan designed the cover art for this poetry anthology. He loves to draw and sit calmly on a chair next to a window relaxing and drinking in the brown, sweet smell and the bitter smoke coming from his cup of coffee.

He who crossed the border safely. He who was like a feathered wing, floating in the wind.

Thanh Tran was born in Tien Giang City, a small town in the south of Vietnam on the banks of the Mekong Delta. He is 18 years old. He arrived in the U.S. in 2018 when he was fifteen years old. People often mistake him for Chinese because of his almond shaped eyes, eyes that are in love with so many people. Thanh is a person who works and studies like a robot with no rest and no emotions. He works hard every day and every night. When Thanh sees a negative situation he avoids it and stays away. He came to the U.S. because his family needed to make a better life. In Vietnam, Thanh

struggled to learn from the teachers in his school because they taught at a very high level and it was difficult to follow. He was never lazy, he just ran behind because of the way the teachers were teaching. Also, studying in Vietnam would not lead to the future Thanh hopes to have for himself. He watched how his brother learned very well in the Vietnamese school and then went on to graduate from university. But, when his brother graduated, he could only find work doing nails. Thanh is waiting for the time when he will graduate from high school and can go to college and university. He knows that studying will help him change his future and he also thinks that studying in the U.S. is more fun than in Vietnam which makes him want to continue, no matter how much time it takes.

He whose eyes are almond shaped and whose heart has many dreams.

Tieda Tsegay Araya was born on March 20, 2005. She was born in Senafe, the southern region of Eritrea, but she grew up in Asmara. She grew up hearing more than ten languages slapping her ears, but she speaks three languages - Italian, Eritrean and Arabic like mixed like ingredients in one hot dish! But, that's not her fault, it's the empire's fault! Tieda means "respect for the Holy Christ of the cross" and it also means "respect for society."

She who has seen the world's shadow part, so she is thankful for her life being in the world's bright part.

Uyen Cill-Pame was born in Viet Nam at Khanh Hoa. She moved to the USA when she was twelve years old. She speaks and understands two languages, Vietnamese and English. Her favorite colors are black and also white because it is bright and clear. Uyen loves to play badminton with her family and spend time together with them. She misses her home country. Uyen thinks people should plant gardens. She really likes cats and at home she has two cats, their names are Gummy and Bear. She misses her family from Vietnam and she misses the Asian food she loves.

She who misses going to her grandmother's house on Tet.

Yasin Saed is fourteen years old. He was born in Somalia in a small town called Sako. He came to the U.S. in 2018 when he was eleven. He speaks Swahili and English. He likes to help his parents and people and kids. He wants to help the children sleeping outside in Somalia and hopes that someday he can. Yasin dreams of having his own school in Somalia. He traveled from Somalia to Ethiopia and then to Kampala, Uganda to get to the U.S. Yasin loves playing soccer and video games. He also dreams of helping his country, Somalia, and the Somali children.

He who makes chapatti for his little brothers; he who tried to chase after the moon.

Zahra Ahmadi is 17 years old. She was born and raised in Afghanistan. She came to the U.S. in October, 2019 for her education. She can speak three languages—Dari, Turkish and English. Her biggest dream is to be able to go back to her country one day and help those children that are not lucky like her to have their ideal education. She is very thankful for her mom, because she taught her important things that she could never learn by herself. Her name from Arabic means "brightness."

She who speaks in poetry for justice and dreams of peace returning to her homeland.

INDEX